SPORTS in
AMERICA
1990–2003

BOB WOODS

SERIES FOREWORD BY LARRY KEITH

®

Facts On File, Inc.

1990–2003
Sports in America

Facts On File, Inc.
132 West 31st Street
New York NY 10001

Library of Congress Cataloging-in-Publication Data

Sports in America / produced by the Shoreline Publishing Group.
    v. cm.
Includes bibliographical references and indexes.
Contents: [1] 1910-1919 / by James Buckley, Jr. and John Walters — [2] 1920-1939 / by John Walters — [3] 1940-1949 / by Phil Barber — [4] 1950-1959 / by Jim Gigliotti — [5] 1960-1969 / by David Fischer — [6] 1970-1979 / by Timothy J. Seeberg and Jim Gigliotti — [7] 1980-1989 / by Michael Teitelbaum — [8] 1990-1999 / by Bob Woods.

ISBN 0-8160-5233-6 (hc : set : alk. paper) — ISBN 0-8160-5234-4 (hc : v. 1 : alk. paper) — ISBN 0-8160-5235-2 (hc : v. 2 : alk. paper) — ISBN 0-8160-5236-0 (hc : v. 3 : alk. paper) — ISBN 0-8160-5237-9 (hc : v. 4 : alk. paper) — ISBN 0-8160-5238-7 (hc : v. 5 : alk. paper) — ISBN 0-8160-5239-5 (hc : v. 6 : alk. paper) — ISBN 0-8160-5240-9 (hc : v. 7 :alk. paper) — ISBN 0-8160-5241-7 (hc : v. 8 : alk. paper)

1. Sports—United States—History.   I. Buckley, James, 1963-   . II. Shoreline Publishing Group. III. Facts on File, Inc.

GV583.S6826 2004
796'.0973'0904—dc22

                                                                                          2004004276

Facts On File books are available at special discounts when purchased in bulk quantities for businesses, associations, institutions, or sales promotions. Please call our Special Sales Department in New York at (212) 967-8800 or (800) 322-8755.

You can find Facts On File on the World Wide Web at http://www.factsonfile.com

Produced by the Shoreline Publishing Group LLC
Editorial Director: James Buckley Jr.
Contributing Editors: Beth Adelman, Jim Gigliotti
Text design by Thomas Carling, Carling Design, Inc.
Cover design by Pehrsson Design and Cathy Rincon
Index by Nanette Cardon, IRIS

Photo credits: Page 1: Courtesy Sports Immortals, Inc. Pictured are a ticket and program from the September 6, 1995, game in which Baltimore Orioles shortstop Cal Ripken, Jr., broke Lou Gehrig's record for consecutive games played. The jersey comes from the 1995 season, and the ball was autographed by Ripken. For more on this historic event, please see page 54. All interior photos courtesy AP/Wide World except for the following: Corbis: 19, 27, 47, 83, 93.

Printed in the United States of America.

VH PKG 10 9 8 7 6 5 4 3 2 1

This book is printed on acid-free paper.

CONTENTS

Annika Sorenstam (see page 94)

FOREWORD

BY LARRY KEITH

IN THE FALL OF 1984, STUDENTS AT COLUMBIA University's prestigious Graduate School of Journalism requested that a new course be added to the curriculum—sports journalism.

Sports journalism? In the graduate program of an Ivy League institution? Get serious.

But the students were serious, and, as students will do, they persisted. Eventually, the school formed a committee to interview candidates for the position of "adjunct professor." As it happened, though, the committee wasn't just looking for a professional sports journalist to teach the course part time. That august body wanted to hear clear and convincing arguments that the course should be offered at all.

In other words, did sports matter? And, more to the point, should an institution that administered the Pulitzer Prize, the highest award in journalism, associate itself with the coverage of "fun and games?"

Two decades later, I am pleased to say that Columbia did decide to offer the course and that it remains in the curriculum. With modest pride, I confess that I helped make the arguments that swayed the committee and became the new adjunct professor.

I reflected on that experience when the *Sports in America* editors invited me to write the Foreword to this important series. I said then, and I say now, "Sport is an integral part of American society and requires the attention of a competent and vigilant press." For our purposes here, I might also add, "because it offers insights to our history and culture."

Sports in America is much more than a compilation of names, dates, and facts. Each volume chronicles accomplishments, advances, and expansions of the possible. Not just in the physical ability to run faster, jump higher, or hit a ball farther, but in the cognitive ability to create goals and analyze how to achieve them. In this way, sports, the sweaty offspring of recreation and competition, resemble any

other field of endeavor. I certainly wouldn't equate the race for a gold medal with the race to the moon, but the essentials are the same: the application of talent, determination, research, practice, and hard work to a meaningful objective.

Sports matter because they represent the best and worst of us. They give us flesh-and-blood examples of courage and skill. They often embody a heroic human interest story, about overcoming poverty, injustice, injury, or disease. The phrase, "Sports is a microcosm of life," could also be, "Life is a microcosm of sports." Consider racial issues, for example. When Jackie Robinson of the Brooklyn Dodgers broke through Major League Baseball's color barrier in 1947, the significance extended beyond the national pastime. Precisely because baseball *was* the national pastime, this important event reverberated throughout American society.

To be sure, black stars from individual sports had preceded him (notably Joe Louis in boxing and Jesse Owens in track and field), and others would follow (Arthur Ashe in tennis and Tiger Woods in golf), but Robinson stood out as an important member of a *team*. He wasn't just playing with the Dodgers, he was traveling with them, dressing with them, eating with them, living with them. The benefits of integration, the recognition of its humanity, could be appreciated far beyond the borough of Brooklyn.

Sports have always been a laboratory for social issues. Robinson integrated big-league box scores eight years before the U.S. Supreme Court ordered the integration of public schools. Women's official debut in the Olympic Games, though limited to swimming, came in 1912, seven years before they got the right to vote. So even if these sports were late in opening their doors, in another way they were ahead of their time. And if it was necessary to break down some of those doors—Title IX support since 1972 for female college athletics comes to mind—so be it.

Another area of social importance, particularly as it affects young people, is substance abuse. High school, college, and professional teams are united in their opposition to the illegal use of drugs, tobacco, and alcohol. In most venues, testing is mandatory and tolerance is zero. Perhaps the most celebrated case occurred at the 1988 Olympic Games, when Canada's Ben Johnson surrendered his 100-meter gold medal after failing a drug test. Some athletes have lost their careers, and even their lives, to substance abuse. Other athletes have used their fame and success to caution young people about submitting to peer pressure and making poor choices.

Fans care about sports and sports personalities because they provide entertainment and identity. But they aren't the only ones who root, root, root for the home team. Government bodies come on board because sports spur local economies. When a city council votes to help underwrite the cost of a stadium or give financial advantages to the owners of a team, it affects the pocketbook of every taxpayer, not to mention the local ecosystem. When high schools and colleges allocate significant resources to athletics, administrators believe they are serving the greater good, but at what cost? These decisions are relevant far beyond the sports page.

In World War II, America's sporting passion inspired President Franklin Roosevelt to say professional games should not be cancelled. He felt the benefits to the national psyche outweighed the security risk of gathering huge crowds at central locations. In 2001, another generation of fans also continued to attend large-scale sports events because to do otherwise would "let the terrorists win." Being there, yelling your lungs out, cheering victory and bemoaning defeat, is a cleansing, even therapeutic exercise. The security check at the gate is just another price of stepping inside.

Unfortunately, there's a downside to all this. The notion that "Sports build character" is better expressed "Sports *reveal* character." We've witnessed too many coaches and athletes break the rules of fair play and good conduct, on and off the field. We've even seen violence and cheating in youth sports, often by parents of a (supposed) future superstar. We've watched fans "celebrate" championships with destructive behavior. I would argue, however, that these flaws are the exception, not the rule, that the good of sports outweighs the bad, that many of life's success stories took root on an athletic field.

Any serious examination of sports leads, inevitably, to the question of athletes as role models. Pro basketball star Charles Barkley created quite a stir in 1993 when he declared in a Nike shoe commercial, "I am not paid to be a role model." The knee-jerk response was, "But kids look up to you!" Barkley was right to raise the issue, though. He was saying that, in making lifestyle choices in language, clothing, and behavior, young people should look elsewhere for role models—ideally in their own home, to responsible parents.

The fact remains, however, that athletes occupy an exalted place in our society, at least when they are magnified in the mass media, and especially in the big-business, money-motivated sports. The athletes we venerate can be as young as a high school basketball player or as old as a Hall of Famer. (They can even be dead, as Babe Ruth's commercial longevity attests.) They are honored and coddled in a way few mortals are. We are quick—too quick—to excuse their excesses and ignore their indulgences. They influence the way we live (the food on our table, the cars in our driveway) and think (Ted Williams inspired patriotism as a fighter pilot during World War II and the Korean conflict; Muhammad Ali's opposition to the Vietnam War on religious grounds, validated by the Supreme Court, inspired the peace movement). No wonder we elect them—track stars, football coaches, baseball pitchers—to represent us in government. Meanwhile, television networks pay exorbitant sums to sports leagues so their teams can pay fortunes for players' services.

It has always been this way. If we, as a nation, love sports, then we, quite naturally, will love the men and women who play them best. In return, they give us entertainment, release, and inspiration. From the beginning of the 20th century until now, *Sports in America* is their story—and ours.

Larry Keith is a former writer and editor at Sports Illustrated. *He covered baseball and college basketball and edited the official Olympic programs in 1996, 2000 and 2002. He is a former adjunct professor of sports journalism at Columbia University and is a member of the Board of Visitors of the University of North Carolina School of Journalism.*

INTRODUCTION
1990–2003

America enjoyed a period of relative peace and prosperity during the final decade of the 20th century. There were nostalgic efforts to cling to the past, such as baseball's new "retro" ballparks that called to mind the playing fields of earlier years, and the revival of bell-bottom pants in the fashion world, but also an eagerness to blast high-speed into the new millennium along the information superhighway. Alarming news of AIDS, terrorism, and homelessness was often drowned out by the sirens of pop celebrity. Even the Persian Gulf War of 1991 generated an uplifting spin. It was especially evident at the star-spangled Super Bowl XXV in Tampa, Florida, where patriotism packed more punch than the Buffalo Bills' offense.

The first President George Bush couldn't win the battle against economic woes, however, and the nation moved into eight colorful, if controversial, years under Bill Clinton. About the same time that Wall Street's bulls started running wild and the economy skyrocketed, spurred by high-flying dotcom stocks, Chicago's Bulls, behind the gravity-defying feats of Michael Jordan, won the first of their six National Basketball Association (NBA) titles in the 1990s. Reflecting the go-go decade, Air Jordan was equally admired for his commercial endorsements, hugely popular sneaker brand, and ranking atop *Forbes Magazine's* list of richest athletes.

The rite of calling sports a selfish business and referring to athletes as pampered brats dates back to ancient times, when Greek senators cried foul over paying "amateur" Olympians and shut down the original Games because of corruption. In the 1990s, however, the volume of complaints went way up. Free agency, which enabled players to sign with any team, left fans rooting for uniforms rather than the millionaire players in them. The cliché "the best team money can buy" was put to work by George Steinbrenner, Wayne Huizenga, Daniel Snyder, and other wealthy owners. Kids bounded straight from high school to the NBA, and underclassmen left college in droves for the National Football League (NFL). And, incredibly—for the first time since 1904—the World Series was cancelled in 1994 because striking players couldn't agree with stubborn owners on how to divvy up billions of dollars.

The thud of sports heroes falling grew louder, too. O.J. Simpson ran from the law

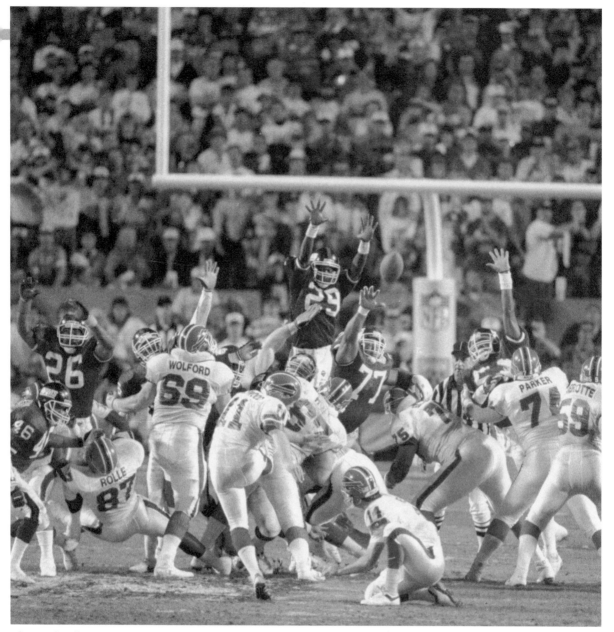

Rise and Fall *Super Bowl XXV lifted Americans' spirits—except for Bills' fans, who lamented Scott Norwood's miss.*

instead of tacklers and Mike Tyson raged inside a jail cell rather than a boxing ring, reminding us just how fragile are our anointed champions. We may have wagged our fingers, but still, we couldn't turn away. Scandal fed the public's appetite for controversy and the media's rush to cover it. The decade witnessed everything from President Clinton versus Monica Lewinsky to Nancy Kerrigan

1990–2003

versus Tonya Harding (see page 45). Early in the 2000s, another media frenzy broke out as NBA superstar Kobe Bryant was accused of rape and his trial approached (see page 100).

In the process, television's reach expanded exponentially. Along with 24-hour general news, sports, weather, and entertainment, cable TV carved such niches as The Golf Channel, SpeedVision, and Court TV. The networks fought tooth and nail for the chance to shell out obscene amounts of money for the broadcast rights to sporting events, regardless of the fact that viewership numbers kept dropping. To pay those bills, and the sports announcers' gigantic salaries, they sold sponsorships to kickoffs, halftime shows, pitching changes, and anything else that could feature a corporate logo.

While cynicism, shame, and greed ran rampant throughout the 1990s, sports fans did have plenty to honestly cheer about. Among the highlights: Bonnie Blair's five Olympic gold medals in speed-skating, Cal Ripken Jr.'s streak of consecutive baseball games played, Greg LeMond's three-peat in the Tour de France bicycle race, John Elway's back-to-back Super Bowl wins, Christian Laettner's miraculous basketball shot on the way to the college championship, Dale Earnhardt's first Daytona 500 victory, the New York Rangers' Stanley Cup win to snap a 53-year drought, sprinter Michael Johnson's unprecedented Olympic double, Tiger Woods' obliteration of the Augusta golf course, and Mark McGwire's 70th home run.

Sports and society connected in other ways in the decade. Though American society as a whole had come a long way in addressing racial inequities by 1990, lingering issues gained attention via the sports world. Shoal Creek Country Club's admission of its first African-American member that year—only under extreme pressure—and the fuss over Woods' arrival on the pro golf scene in 1996 only magnified how much the game of golf

LeMond for "Le Monde" *In the annual Tour de France cycling race, American Greg LeMond provided some of the most thrilling and courageous moments in American sports during the 1990s.*

remained starkly white. On the other hand, just as the O.J. Simpson trial exposed a rift between blacks and whites, baseball's celebration of the 50th anniversary of Jackie Robinson's major league debut provided some healing.

Women overwhelmingly proved their place in sports during the 1990s. Increased opportunities and funding for women's high school and college sports programs, federally mandated by Title IX in 1975, reaped rewards with Olympic championships in soccer, volleyball, and softball. The U.S. soccer team won two of the first three World Cups for women, including a thrilling tournament on American turf in 1999. And women's basketball hit the big time, exemplified by outstanding college teams at the University of Connecticut and the University of Tennessee, where individuals such as Rebecca Lobo and Chamique Holdsclaw gained superstar status. Women literally "got game" when the NBA spun off the Women's National Basketball Association in 1997.

As the country headed into the uncharted waters of the 21st century, it could turn, as past generations always have, to sports and athletes for inspiration. "The spirit, the will to win, and the will to excel are the things that endure," said Vince Lombardi, the late, great football coach and motivator. "These qualities are so much more important than the events that occur."

That indomitable spirit came shining through when one-handed baseball pitcher Jim Abbott threw a no-hitter, when speed skater Dan Jansen picked himself up after falling in races time and time

Women Go Pro *The continuing rise of women in sports was signaled with the debut of the Women's National Basketball Association in 1997. Nykesha Sales of the Connecticut Sun was one of several players who gained national stardom.*

again until he won a gold medal, and when cancer survivor Lance Armstrong captured cycling's grueling Tour de France. Their courage and perseverance gave everyone hope that greatness can still be achieved.

1990

Bo Knows Rose Bowl Woes

When he awoke on January 1, Glenn "Bo" Schembechler's (b.1929) New Year's resolution might have been to close out his illustrious 27-year career as a college football coach smelling like a rose. Instead, the bloom came off a not-so-grand finale. That afternoon, his University of Michigan Wolverines (10–1) lined up against the University of Southern California (USC) Trojans (8–2–1) in the 76th annual Rose Bowl in Pasadena, California. It marked the 10th time since 1969 that Schembechler had led his team to this bowl game between the Big Ten and Pac Ten champions. Yet he'd only won twice— following the 1980 and 1988 seasons. In that second win, he beat the Trojans.

This USC squad featured rookie sensation quarterback Todd Marinovich. His 22-of-31 passing performance, coupled with Pasadena-born running back Ricky Ervins' 126 rushing yards, eventually overcame a valiant Michigan effort.

With 12 minutes remaining in the game, the score was tied at 10–10. Michigan's defense had held USC to 27 third-quarter yards, and now the offense had the ball on its own 46-yard line, with mo-

mentum seemingly on Schembechler's side. There was a growing sense among the sold-out crowd of 103,450 that the Wolverines might soon be carrying their coach off the field on their victorious shoulders and into a glorious sunset.

Just like that, though, a holding penalty on a fake punt play nullified a would-be first down for the Wolverines. Michigan was forced to punt—for real. The Trojans chewed up yardage and the clock on their next possession. They marched 75 yards in 13 plays, culminated with a 14-yard, game-winning touchdown run by Ervins with 1:10 left.

Even in his eighth Rose Bowl defeat, Schembechler made the final walk off the football field with his head held high. The Wolverines had their first 10-win season since 1986 and earned their second consecutive outright Big Ten championship. After 21 seasons in Ann Arbor, Schembechler retired as the winningest coach in Michigan football history, with a 194–48–5 record. He went out a winner.

The Fall of Tyson, Part I

 Few people outside the boxing world had ever heard of James "Buster"

Buster Who? *Mike Tyson (on the mat) was invincible until he ran into the relatively unknown Buster Douglas.*

Douglas (b.1960) before February 11. And even those familiar with the sport didn't give the 6-foot-4, 230-pound fighter much of a chance against heavyweight champion Mike Tyson (b.1966). After all, the ferocious "Iron Mike" was undefeated in 37 bouts, winning 33 by knockouts. His opponents were lucky to last beyond the first round. So when Douglas stepped into the ring that night in Tokyo, Japan, it was no surprise that he was a 42–1 underdog. The surprise came a bit later.

Early on, it became apparent that this fight would not be another typical Tyson demolition job. The much bigger Douglas used his incredible 13-inch reach advan-

Media Milestones

✔ On January 31, *The National Sports Daily*, America's first all-sports newspaper, made its debut in New York, Chicago, and Los Angeles. Edited by Frank Deford, it folded in 18 months.

✔ NBC did not stand for Notre Dame Broadcasting Company, even though the network signed a five-year, $30-million deal to broadcast 30 University of Notre Dame home football games from 1991 to 1995.

✔ In March, CBS renewed its NFL contract, paying more than $1 billion to telecast National Football Conference (NFC) games for four more years, as well as the 1992 Super Bowl. A day later, NBC paid $752 million for four more years of American Football Conference (AFC) games and the 1993 Super Bowl.

✔ On April Fool's Day, CBS fired broadcaster Brent Musburger after 15 years with the network, but did allow him to broadcast the National Collegiate Athletic Association (NCAA) men's basketball championship game the next day. A month later, he signed a six-year deal with ABC Sports.

✔ Al Michaels became the highest-paid television sportscaster by signing a five-year contract with ABC for $2.5 million a year.

✔ In October, the long-time radio play-by-play broadcaster for basketball's Boston Celtics, Johnny Most, retired at the age of 67.

With a relentless combination of punches, Douglas sent Tyson tumbling down. The champ stumbled to his feet, but was clearly dazed. The referee stopped the fight and declared Douglas the winner and new champion. Boxing commentator Larry Merchant said afterward, "The Japanese people came to see Godzilla, only the wrong person turned out to be Godzilla." It remains one of the greatest upsets in sports history—even more so considering that Douglas' unexpected reign ended just eight and a half months later, when he lost his only title defense to Evander Holyfield.

The Terrific Twins of Lacrosse

The undefeated Syracuse University men's lacrosse team thumped Loyola College, 21–9, for its third straight NCAA championship on May 28. So why all the long faces on the Syracuse Orangemen? Simple: The game marked the end of the magnificent Gait Brothers era.

The tandem talents of identical twins Gary and Paul Gait (b.1967), seniors on the Orange lacrosse squad, produced one of the most dynamic duos in collegiate sports history. In that lopsided championship contest—both the goal total and margin of victory set NCAA finals records—they scored eight goals and finished their four-year careers with a combined 319 goals and 146 assists. In the three games Syracuse played in the 1990 postseason, Gary's nine goals established the record for the most ever scored in the NCAA tournament. He also owns another NCAA record for the most goals scored in a single game

tage and lightning jab effectively to stun the 5-foot-11 Tyson. A punishing right wobbled Iron Mike in the fifth round and raised a welt over his left eye. The champ grew increasingly frustrated. Still, he battled back, and late in the eighth round he caught Douglas with a vicious uppercut that dropped the challenger to the canvas. Douglas barely recovered, rising at the count of nine.

The 10th round will go down in history as one of boxing's most memorable.

(nine), in a May 1988 shellacking of Navy.

The Gaits' stick handling, passing, shooting, and overall athleticism dazzled fans and befuddled opponents with moves that had never been seen before. In one, a lacrosse version of basketball's alley-oop play, Paul would lob a high pass to Gary as he streaked across the front of the goal. Gary cradled the ball above his head, and while still airborne and with his back to the mouth of the goal, he would bring his stick down and whip the ball between his legs and into the net.

More spectacular was Gary's jaw-dropping "Air Gait" play, first witnessed during an NCAA championship semifinal match in 1988 against the University of Pennsylvania. Cradling the ball behind the Penn goal and just outside the protective crease, Gary leapt toward the front of the net. He flew over the goal, angled his stick in front of it, and, using the crossbar as a fulcrum, jammed the ball into the net—the equivalent of lacrosse's first slam dunk.

Invented centuries ago by Native Americans, lacrosse has a storied history at Syracuse. Jim Brown (b.1936), who played football at Syracuse and later for the Cleveland Browns, also starred on the university's lacrosse team (as well as its track and basketball teams) in the mid-1950s. He is still regarded as one of the best collegiate lacrosse players ever. Since 1971, when the NCAA added lacrosse to its roster of sanctioned sports, Syracuse has won eight championships. A true dynasty, the Orangemen advanced to the final game every year from 1983 to 2002.

The brothers Gait went on to record-setting careers in professional lacrosse, and remain instrumental in promoting the sport in youth and high school programs. Two ironic footnotes: Syracuse's 1990 championship was later voided due to violations of NCAA rules, and the "Air Gait" move was deemed illegal when the NCAA banned players from diving into the crease.

Bad Boys Do Good in NBA Title Repeat

The Detroit Pistons had finally reached the NBA mountaintop in 1989, winning a championship for the first time in the franchise's 41-year history. Yet critics wondered if their four-game sweep of the Los Angeles Lakers in the best-of-seven-games NBA Finals had more to do with hamstring injuries to L.A.'s Earvin "Magic" Johnson (b.1959) and Byron Scott than a truly outstanding Pistons team. Were they merely a one-year wonder?

The Pistons silenced the critics with a hard-fought defense of their championship in June, beating the Portland Trail Blazers, four games to one. In the process, Detroit joined the Lakers and Boston Celtics as the only teams in NBA history to win consecutive titles.

The 1989–1990 Pistons reflected the tough, hard-working personality of the Motor City. Head coach Chuck Daly (b.1930) preached defense, and his players heeded his words well—sometimes too well, other teams charged. With an aggressive, hard-fouling, in-your-face style, they became known as the NBA's Bad Boys.

Call them what you will, the Pistons had the league's stingiest defense, holding

1990

opponents to 98.3 points per game and a .447 shooting percentage.

Daly made up for the off-season loss of power forward and chief enforcer Rick Mahorn to the expansion Minnesota Timberwolves by moving James Edwards and Dennis Rodman (b.1961) into the starting rotation opposite bruising center Bill Laimbeer. All-star point guard Isiah

Point Man *Point guard Isiah Thomas was the man who made the Pistons go. He earned MVP honors in Detroit's five-game victory over Portland in the NBA Finals.*

Thomas (b.1961), Joe Dumars, and Vinnie "the Microwave" Johnson propelled a lethal outside shooting game. Detroit finished the season with an Eastern Conference-best record of 59–23, highlighted by a 25–1 streak running from January to March.

The Trail Blazers pulled into suburban Detroit's Palace of Auburn Hills for game one of the finals with an identical won-lost record. Led by high-flying scoring machine Clyde Drexler (averaging 23.3 points per game, point guard Terry Porter, and power forward Buck Williams, Portland wasn't about to roll over for the Bad Boys. In fact, their intensity on both ends of the court caught the Pistons by surprise for three quarters, and the Trailblazers led, 90–80, with seven minutes left in the game.

That's the point at which Thomas took over. His offensive outburst, featuring a seven-point barrage, inspired the defense, which made huge stops and forced turnovers. A pair of Thomas three-point baskets sparked a come-from-behind, 105–99 victory. "We were dead in the water, belly up," Daly said after the game. "It was just a special player making great shots."

Game two in Detroit turned into another tight affair. Despite an inspired second-half effort by Laimbeer—he scored 19 points in the last 17 minutes—the game went into overtime. With four seconds left in overtime, Laimbeer hit the last of his six three-pointers, tying an NBA Finals record, to put the Pistons up by one. But Drexler was fouled by Rodman with two seconds remaining and coolly swished both free throws. The Trailblazers escaped with a 106–105 win, taking away Detroit's home-court advantage and sending the series to Portland's Memorial Coliseum for the next three games.

The Pistons hadn't won a game at the Portland Coliseum in 17 years, and they were without the services of NBA Defensive Player of the Year Rodman, who was out with an ankle injury. Those obstacles didn't seem to matter as Detroit's offense caught fire. No one was hotter than Dumars, who scored 33 points. The Microwave sizzled with 21 points, and the home team got smoked, 121–106.

Both teams ran hot and cold in game four. Portland raced to a 32–22 first-quarter lead, but scored only 14 points in the second period and was down 51–46 at the half. Thomas poured in 22 points in the third period, then the Trailblazers countered with a 28–11 run to take a 93–92 lead with 5:20 left in the game. A see-saw battle ensued down the stretch, until the Pistons were up by three points with 1.8 seconds on the clock. A 35-foot shot by Portland's Danny Young went in, but the referees concluded that time had run out before he took the shot.

Portland, trying to become the first NBA team to come back from a 3–1 deficit in the finals, led by eight points with 10 minutes to play in game five. Johnson heated up again, however, scoring 16 points and lifting Detroit to a 90–90 tie in the final seconds. To cap off his scintillating performance, the Microwave sank a 15-footer with 0:00.7 showing on the clock. Portland's goose was officially cooked. The Pistons won, 92–90.

Despite his teammates' heroics, Thomas received the series' Most Valuable

An American in Paris
Again and Again and Again

On July 22, Greg LeMond pedaled his bicycle down Paris' Champs-Elysées, wearing a yellow jersey and a triumphant, if weary, smile. He had just won his second straight Tour de France, and his third since 1986—when he became the first American to win the grueling three-week, 2,500-mile bicycle race.

Born on June 26, 1961, in Lakeland, California, Gregory James LeMond got hooked on cycling when he was 14 years old. The word "obsessed" might be more accurate, considering that he dropped out of high school to take up the sport professionally. He earned a spot on the U.S. national cycling team and eventually moved to Europe, where cycling is much more popular than in the United States, to train and compete. His countless hours of hard work paid off in 1986, when he beat out his mentor and teammate, the French cycling idol Bernard Hinault, himself a five-time Tour de France winner.

Less than a year later, LeMond was accidentally shot while hunting in California and nearly died. Throughout his long and painful rehabilitation, LeMond vowed to compete again in the Tour de France. Miraculously, he lined up for the start of the 1989 race, which is run in 21 day-long stages ranging from 100 to 155 miles each. He overcame a seemingly insurmountable lead by Frenchman Laurent Fignon to win by eight seconds, the closest finish ever in the Tour de France's 85-year history. He was named *Sports Illustrated's* 1989 Sportsman of the Year.

In 1990, LeMond was consistent rather than spectacular. He didn't take the lead until after the 20th stage, then rode to a relatively easy win over Italy's Claudio Chiapucci by 2:16.

Player trophy. Along with sinking 11 of 16 shots from three-point range, he averaged 27.6 points, eight assists, and 5.2 rebounds in the five games.

"You can say what you want about me," the flashy leader of the Bad Boys remarked, "but you can't say that I'm not a winner."

1990

A Course of a Different Color

Slavery ended in the United States in 1862, yet it took more than 100 years for Congress to pass the Civil Rights Act of 1964, outlawing discrimination based on race, color, religion, or national origin. And it took another 26 years for Shoal Creek Country Club in Birmingham, Alabama, to grant membership to an African American. And that came about only after Shoal Creek's policy of no black members was exposed shortly before the club was set to host the Professional Golfers' Association (PGA) 1990 Championship. The policy sparked a nationwide controversy and forced the change.

Birmingham had been the center of racial upheaval in 1963, when police attacked civil rights demonstrators with dogs and fire hoses. And while race relations in the United States had greatly improved by 1990 in many areas—including education, employment, and business opportunities—private golf clubs throughout the country remained largely whites-only bastions. Many didn't permit women, Jews, Hispanics, or other minorities to join, either. Such exclusionary rules were seldom challenged or even publicized—until Shoal Creek.

In late June, two months before the PGA Championship, the *Birmingham Post-Herald* ran a story about Shoal Creek. Quoted in the article, its founder, Hall Thompson, stated flatly, "This country club is our home and we pick and choose whom we want. . . . I think we've said that we don't discriminate in every other area except the blacks." Thompson apologized later for his remarks, but he didn't retract them.

Overnight, outrage and protest erupted. The word quickly spread, too, that Shoal Creek was hardly alone. Of the 39 PGA Tour events in 1990, at least 17 had been or were to be held at clubs with no black members, the *Charlotte Observer* reported. The United States Golf Association (USGA), which runs the U.S. Open, had scheduled four of the next five Opens at all-white clubs. Suddenly, the golf establishment's dirty laundry was hung out for all to see.

Protests demanding that the PGA move the tournament to another site went unheeded at first, as did calls for Shoal Creek to drop its racist policy. There was only one black professional golfer on the Tour then, so there wasn't much dissent from the players' ranks. That all changed, however, when IBM, Toyota, Sharp Electronics, and other advertisers threatened to pull out of the PGA Championship broadcast on ABC and ESPN. Before long, Shoal Creek admitted its first black member, and the PGA Tour announced that it would no longer hold tournaments at clubs that discriminate. Similar standards were soon adopted by the USGA and the Ladies Professional Golf Association (LPGA).

The actual tournament in August, nearly a footnote amid the turmoil, eventually was won by Wayne Grady. The Australian shot a four-round total of 282 and edged American Fred Couples by three strokes; Couples bogeyed (shot one over par) four straight holes on the last nine holes of the course to see his championship hopes slip away.

Other Milestones of 1990

✔ Super Bowl XXIV on January 28 was a super blowout, as the San Francisco 49ers corralled the Denver Broncos, 55–10, behind a record five touchdown passes by quarterback Joe Montana, who was named Most Valuable Player.

✔ Major League Baseball owners locked out players from spring training for 32 days in March and April, delaying the start of the regular season by one week.

✔ Loyola Marymount University's All-America basketball forward Hank Gathers died of heart failure after collapsing on the court during a West Coast Conference tournament game on March 7.

✔ In her professional debut in March, 13-year-old Jennifer Capriati reached the finals of the Virginia Slims tennis tournament.

✔ The University of Wisconsin's Suzy Favor won the 800-meter and 1,500-meter races at the NCAA Track and Field Championships in March, giving her nine individual titles and making her the winningest athlete in NCAA history.

✔ In the most lopsided victory ever in an NCAA men's basketball championship game, the University of Nevada-Las Vegas whipped Duke University on April 2, 103–73.

Ken Griffey Sr. and Ken Griffey Jr.

✔ Oakland A's outfielder Jose Canseco signed a new contract that made him the first baseball player to earn more than $5 million a year.

✔ On June 10, 16-year-old Monica Seles became the youngest player ever to win tennis' French Open.

✔ On July 24, baseball's all-time hits leader, Pete Rose, was sentenced to federal prison for five months and fined $50,000 for income tax evasion.

✔ On August 31, Ken Griffey Sr. and Jr. became the first father and son to play Major League Baseball together on the same team when they took the field for the Seattle Mariners against the Kansas City Royals.

Little Leaguers of the Far East

Baseball may be America's pastime, but don't tell that to Little Leaguers in Taiwan. In Williamsport, Pennsylvania, where the sport's truly world series is played annually among teams from around the globe, the 1990 Little League Championship was won by Taiwan, which shut out the team from Shippensburg, Pennsylvania, 9–0, in the August final.

The win was no fluke, either. Taiwan obliterated its three opponents in the tournament by a combined tally of 43–1. The championship was Taiwan's 14th in the last 22 years. "The game of baseball is very beautiful," said manager Wang Tzyy-Tsann. "You can play it to perfection if you pay attention to the fundamentals."

1991

Wide Right

Super Bowl XXV will forever be summed up by two words: wide right. But depending on whether you're a fan of the New York Giants or the Buffalo Bills, they're famous or infamous. Hearing them will make you either stand up and cheer or break down and cry.

On January 27, with eight seconds left in the closest Super Bowl ever played, the Giants led, 20–19. Bills kicker Scott Norwood, with the ball on New York's 47-yard line, trotted onto the field to attempt a game-winning field goal. Adam Lingner snapped the ball and holder Frank Reich placed it cleanly on the grass. Norwood ran up to it, swung his right leg, and the ball sailed toward the goal posts. As players on both sidelines watched (or couldn't) and prayed (that God really does take sides in sports events), the ball strayed to the right. It wound up wide by several feet. The game was over; the Giants had won. The thrill of victory, the agony of defeat.

This agony-and-ecstasy ending was only fitting, considering the stark contrast between the Giants and the Bills when they arrived at Tampa Stadium in Tampa, Florida, on what was already unlike any previous Super Sunday. The United States was at war with Iraq (see the box on this page), and security at the stadium was extraordinary. So was the outpouring of patriotism among the 73,813 in attendance: American flags waving, chants of "U-S-A" reverberating, fighter jets overhead flying, Whitney Houston's inspiring rendition of the national anthem.

The Giants advanced to the NFL championship game on the strength of their defense, which was the best in the league during the regular season. It would need to be near perfect to counter the NFL's highest-scoring offense, the Bills. New York had given up a total of just 16

The Persian Gulf War

On January 16, Operation Desert Storm went into action in the Middle East. Responding to the surprise invasion of Kuwait by neighboring Iraq and its dictator, Saddam Hussein, on August 2, 1990, an American-led coalition of nations launched a massive air attack aimed at destroying Iraq's military. On February 24, the coalition's ground forces entered Kuwait and southern Iraq. After four intense days of fighting, Iraq was defeated and Kuwait was liberated. There had been some talk of canceling the Super Bowl, but the NFL decided the game should go on.

Be Like Mike   *Chicago Bulls superstar Michael Jordan added an NBA championship to his resumé (see page 21).*

points in its two National Football Conference (NFC) playoff wins, over the Chicago Bears (31–3) and the San Francisco 49ers (15–13); Buffalo had racked up 95 points in beating the Miami Dolphins (44–34) and the Los Angeles Raiders (51–3) for the American Football Conference (AFC) title.

The Giants' game plan hinged on keeping Bills quarterback Jim Kelly (b.1960) and his no-huddle, quick-strike offense off the field for as long as possible. While its defense had to execute flawlessly, the key really was New York's ball-control offense. That meant efficient drives that took a lot of time—combining short passes from quarterback Jeff Hostetler (pressed into service six weeks earlier when starting quarterback Phil Simms injured his shoulder) and a huge effort from running back Otis Anderson.

The Giants maintained possession of the football for a Super Bowl-record 40 minutes, 33 seconds—more than two-thirds of the 60-minute game. Hostetler completed 20 of 32 passes, and Anderson rushed for 102 yards to earn the Most Valuable Player (MVP) award.

1991

Coach K Finally Gets the Big W

For Duke University's men's basketball team and its coach, Mike Krzyzewski (b.1947), April Fool's Day was no joke as Duke won the 1991 NCAA Championship, topping the University of Kansas, 72–65, and making fools of all those who said the Duke Blue Devils couldn't win the big game.

Coach K, as he is known (because his name is difficult to say; it is actually pronounced sheh-SHEFFS-key), had led the Blue Devils to the Final Four three straight years, from 1988 to 1990, as well as in 1986. Each time, they sailed easily enough through the first four rounds of the 64-team NCAA tournament. But they didn't reach the final game until 1990—then only to be embarrassed, 103–73, by the University of Nevada-Las Vegas (UNLV) Running Rebels. So this year, when Duke (26–7) drew unbeaten (30–0) and number-one-ranked UNLV in the semifinals at the Hoosier Dome in Indianapolis, Indiana, Coach K's doubters came out in full force.

Against Player of the Year Larry Johnson, All-America forward Stacey Augmon, and the rest of UNLV coach Jerry Tarkanian's (b.1930) shark attack, the Blue Devils weren't thought to have much of a chance. But with an aggressive, suffocating defense and the offensive talents of its two stars—point guard Bobby Hurley and center Christian Laettner—Duke pulled off one of the tournament's greatest upsets, winning 79–77.

When his team took the floor against the Kansas Jayhawks (22–7) in the finals

on April 3, Coach K wondered if they would have enough energy after the emotional win two nights earlier. The Blue Devils quickly dispelled any doubts, shooting a torrid 59 percent in the first half to take a 42–34 lead at halftime. Hurley and Laettner again propelled the team, with a huge boost off the bench from guard Bill McCaffrey, who scored 16 points.

Kansas, meanwhile, shot inconsistently. Despite a valiant effort in the game's closing minutes, when Duke started to wear down, the Jayhawks couldn't get closer than five points. Duke was crowned national champions, and Coach K won the biggest game of all.

Bittersweet Stanley Cup Victory

The Pittsburgh Penguins of the National Hockey League (NHL) ended 23 years of frustration by winning the team's first Stanley Cup on May 25 at the Met Center in Bloomington, Minnesota. The Penguins trounced the Minnesota North Stars, 8–0, to capture the Cup in game six of the best-of-seven finals. Pittsburgh superstar Mario Lemieux (b.1965), who had missed the first 50 games of the 80-game regular season due to a back injury, received the Conn Smythe Trophy as the MVP of the playoffs.

Lemieux had five goals and seven assists in the finals, despite sitting out game three with back spasms. Since being drafted by the Penguins in 1984, Lemieux had earned the nickname Super Mario by winning two NHL scoring titles and the league's MVP honors in 1988.

As it goes in team sports, though, even the greatest players need support. The Penguins finally surrounded Lemieux with just the right mix of talent for the 1990–1991 season, including rookie Jaromir Jagr, Mark Recchi, Paul Coffey, and goaltender Tom Barasso. Then they brought in coach Bob Johnson, who was executive director of USA Hockey and had led the University of Wisconsin to three NCAA hockey titles, to run the team.

Unfortunately, "Badger," as the coach was affectionately known, couldn't be around to help the Penguins defend their long-awaited Stanley Cup championship. In August, the Penguins' beloved coach was diagnosed with brain cancer. On November 26, six months before his team's triumph, he died.

The Bulls Run with Jordan

Michael Jordan (b.1963) had clearly achieved superstardom in the NBA well before the 1990–1991 season. He reigned supreme as the league's leading scorer all four previous seasons, and earned his first MVP award the year before. Yet as high as Jordan soared, there were always doubts and whispers. Could he lead the Chicago Bulls to an NBA championship?

Resounding cheers drowned out the whispers on June 12 when the Bulls claimed the team's very first NBA title by defeating the Los Angeles Lakers, 108–101, at the Great Western Forum in Los Angeles. Chicago lost the first game in the best-of-seven finals at home, then took four straight. Jordan, who averaged 31.2 points, 11.4 assists, and 6.6 rebounds

Super Mario *Pittsburgh Penguins star Mario Lemieux holds the Stanley Cup aloft after leading his team to the first National Hockey League championship in franchise history.*

per game for the series, was named the MVP—to go along with another regular-season scoring title and MVP trophy.

The finals included a marquee matchup between Jordan and the Lakers' Earvin "Magic" Johnson, owner of five championship rings. Neither superstar disappointed.

While Jordan performed his MVP feats, Johnson tried to carry the Lakers on his back. The 6-foot-9 point guard posted the 29th and 30th triple-doubles (double figures in scoring, rebounds, and assists) of his career, set a five-game finals record

1991

with 62 assists, and averaged 18.6 points and 8 rebounds per game.

Beyond their individual heroics, teamwork made the difference. Scottie Pippen (b.1965), Horace Grant, Bill Cartwright, B.J. Armstrong, and John Paxson provided the complements to Jordan's aerobatics that had been lacking when the Bulls lost the Eastern Conference Championship the previous two seasons. James Worthy, Byron Scott, A.C. Green, and other aging Lakers, meanwhile, couldn't muster the wizardry that had sparked the Lakers' five NBA titles during the 1980s.

The torch had officially been passed. "I'm not even thinking about any other championships right now," Jordan said during the victory celebration. "I just want to enjoy this one for as long as I can."

It's a Bird, It's a Plane . . .

It's Mike Powell (b.1963), soaring to an incredible world record of 29 feet, 4 1/2 inches in the long jump on August 30. By two inches, he broke the 23-year-old mark set by Bob Beamon at the 1968 Summer Olympics in Mexico City— a record many considered unbeatable.

When Powell jogged into a hot and muggy National Stadium in Tokyo for the 1991 World Championships of Track and Field, few expected him to leap into the history books—except Powell, who, for metric-minded Japanese fans, had prophetically signed autographs with "8.95?"—that's meters, and 8.95 meters converts to 29 feet, 4 1/2 inches.

Yet before Powell entertained any thoughts of breaking Beamon's venerable

record, he first had to contend with the here and now: the great Carl Lewis (b.1961). Lewis was not only the fastest man in the world (he set a world record in the 100-meter sprint at the same meet on August 25), but also the owner of back-to-back Olympic gold medals in the long jump at the 1984 and 1988 Games. Indeed, he was undefeated over a 10-year, 65-meet stretch. Powell, the Olympic silver medalist in 1988, hadn't beaten Lewis in 15 tries.

This all must have weighed heavily on Powell's mind, because the first four of his six jumps were relatively short compared to Lewis' efforts; three of Lewis' jumps were at least 29 feet (though he was aided by a wind at his back, so the jumps did not count for the record books). But on Powell's fifth jump, he summoned up every ounce of talent, frustration, and determination—and made the jump of his life.

Even as the crowd cheered the incredible eclipse of Beamon's record, Powell stood nervously awaiting Lewis' final jump. When it came up well short, the world officially had its new long jump superman.

Worst-to-First Double Play

Both the Minnesota Twins and the Atlanta Braves finished dead last in their respective divisions in 1990. And while hope springs eternal at the start of every baseball season, neither team could have anticipated their historic reversal of fortunes in 1991. There they stood, nonetheless, at the end of the 162-game regular season, alive and well in first

Rickey Steals the Show

"Mayday" is the international call for help. Many baseball pitchers must have felt like shouting it whenever they saw Rickey Henderson lurking on first base. So it was only appropriate that on May 1—May Day around the world—Henderson became Major League Baseball's all-time stolen base leader, stealing base number 939 for his Oakland A's against the New York Yankees to break Lou Brock's record in a game at the Oakland-Alameda County Coliseum in California.

Born on Christmas Day in 1958 in Chicago, the gifted Henderson lent his unique package of baseball skills to eight different major league teams over a high-speed career that spanned 25 years in 2003. That included four stints with the Oakland Athletics, with whom he moved up from the minor leagues as a 21-year-old rookie in 1979.

Rickey Henderson

Henderson quickly established himself as a complete, five-tool player: He hit for a high average and with home run power, fielded and threw the ball exceptionally well, and was a demon on the base paths. "He's the best lead-off hitter of all time, no question," former Yankees shortstop Tony Kubek told *The Sporting News* in 1986.

The key for the first batter in the lineup is to get on base, and Henderson mastered the art. A .279 lifetime hitter, he had 3,055 career hits (through 2003). And he was just as happy to draw a walk. He did whatever it took to get on base, as his .401 career on-base percentage testifies.

But it was on base that he was most dangerous. The 10-time All-Star led the American League in stolen bases 12 times, most dramatically in 1982 when he set the single-season record with 130 steals. More than any other major leaguer, he eventually wound up crossing home plate: Henderson holds the record for runs scored, at 2,295. At age 44 in 2003, he played 30 games for the Los Angeles Dodgers. He finished the season at 1,406 career stolen bases—and with a certain pass into the Baseball Hall of Fame.

1991

place—the Twins atop the American League's West Division, the Braves kings of the National League's Western Division. Never before had any major league team gone from worst to first in consecutive seasons, and now two had done it in the same year.

As if those extraordinary dual achievements weren't enough, the two teams survived their league championship series and squared off in October in one of the most closely contested and entertaining World Series of all time.

Seven thrilling games later, heroes had emerged on both sides, like a contest of "anything you can do, I can do better." Four games were decided on the final pitch. Three went into extra innings. Five were decided by a single run.

Game seven, on Sunday night, October 27, at the Hubert H. Humphrey Metrodome in Minneapolis, was a true fall classic. The finale pitted Atlanta's 24-year-old John Smoltz against 36-year-old veteran Jack Morris, both pitching on just three days' rest. They each came out

Other Milestones of 1991

Left to right: Harding, Yamaguchi, and Kerrigan

✔ American women skaters swept the World Figure Skating Championships in Munich, Germany, on March 16. Kristi Yamaguchi won the gold medal, Tonya Harding won the silver, and Nancy Kerrigan won the bronze.

✔ On March 30, the Northern Michigan University Wildcats captured their first NCAA Division I hockey title by

beating the Boston University Terriers, 8–7, in triple overtime in the championship game.

✔ On the same day that Rickey Henderson set his stolen base record (see page 23), May 1, 44-year-old Nolan Ryan pitched his seventh career no-hitter, as the Texas Rangers blanked the Toronto Blue Jays, 3–0, at Arlington Stadium in Arlington, Texas.

✔ Unknown rookie John Daly won the Professional Golfers Association Championship on August 11.

✔ On September 13, at the World Gymnastics Championships in Indianapolis, Kim Zmeskal, 15, became the first American to win the women's all-around title.

✔ NBA star Magic Johnson shocked the sports world on November 7 by announcing his retirement because he had contracted HIV, the virus that causes AIDS.

✔ On December 14, University of Michigan receiver Desmond Howard was awarded the Heisman Trophy as college football's best player for 1991.

strong, throwing shutouts into the eighth inning. It looked like the Braves would score in the top half of the eighth inning, when Terry Pendleton smacked a ball into the gap in left-center field with Lonnie Smith on first base and no outs. But Smith hesitated coming around second base and had to hold up at third. The crafty Morris then pitched his way out of the inning.

The game remained scoreless after nine innings, and Morris kept on pitching—holding Atlanta scoreless in the top of the 10th inning. In the bottom of the inning, with one out and the bases loaded, Minnesota's Gene Larkin hit a fly ball that landed just beyond the infield, scoring Dan Gladden to win the game—and the World Series.

Morris, who won two of his three starts and notched a measly 1.17 earned run average (ERA, calculated by dividing a pitcher's earned runs by the number of innings he pitched, multiplied by nine), was voted MVP of the series. In the end, the worst part was that one team had to lose.

You Goal, Girls!

 Half a world away from home, in Tianhe Stadium in Guangzhou, China, the U.S. women's national soccer team scored two historic firsts on November 30. Its 18 members received gold medals for their victory in the world's first women's World Cup Soccer Championship. They also became the first U.S. world champions in soccer since the game was introduced in America 128 years earlier.

The title came after a heart-stopping 2–1 triumph over Norway. With three minutes remaining and the game tied, U.S. striker Michelle Akers kicked the decisive goal.

Akers (who scored the game's other goal too, giving her a team-high 10 goals in the six-game tournament) earned high praise from soccer legend Pelé, who led Brazil to three World Cup titles (1958, 1962, 1970). "I like her because she is intelligent, has presence of mind, and is often in the right position," he told reporters at the stadium. "She's fantastic."

1992

The Golden Girls

United States Olympians brought home a total of 11 medals from the Games of the XVI Winter Olympiad, held in Albertville, France, February 8 to 23. American women won nine of them, including all five of the United States' gold medals.

Leading the way was speed skater Bonnie Blair (b.1964) of Champaign, Illinois. The youngest in a family of five speed skating kids, she first laced up a pair of hand-me-down skates at the age of two and began competing when she was four.

At the 1988 Winter Olympics in Calgary, Alberta, she not only edged the defending East German champion in the 500-meter race—by two one-hundredths of a second—for the gold, but also set a world record. Blair won the event again in Albertville, by a more "comfortable" 18 one-hundredths of a second. Blair thus became the first U.S. woman to win a gold medal in two Olympics.

Four days later, with "Blair's Bunch" of 50 or so family and hometown friends, including her sponsors from the Champaign Police Department, cheering her on, she took the gold in the 1,000-meter race.

As did Blair growing up, many speed skaters start out racing in short-track competition, which was added to the Olympic slate of events in 1992. In short track, instead of racing in pairs against the clock, skaters race in a tight, bump-and-grind pack, usually four at a time—like roller derby on ice. The first to cross the finish line wins; elimination heats lead to semifinals and finals. In the finals, American Cathy Turner, who had taken an eight-year break from the sport from 1980 to 1988 to pursue a singing career, won the 500-meter race in a photo finish. With China's Li Yan ahead as they approached the finish line, Turner made a final kick and beat Li by four one-hundredths of a second, or about the length of a skate blade.

Kristi Yamaguchi (b.1971) laced up skates at Albertville, too, in the women's figure skating event. She arrived at the Games as one of two favorites, along with Japan's Midori Ito. The media hyped their contrasting styles: The more athletic Ito's repertoire featured explosive jumps; Yamaguchi was more polished and artistic. A former pairs skater who grew up clutch-

Go, Speed Racer *Speed skater Bonnie Blair was one of the American stars at the Winter Olympic Games in Albertville, France.*

ing a Dorothy Hamill doll, Yamaguchi led after the first half of the competition, the short program, in which required moves are performed. Although she fell in the longer freestyle program, Ito did as well, and Yamaguchi skated away with the gold medal.

America's fifth golden girl, Donna Weinbrecht, won her medal on the snow, in a new Olympic sport: freestyle skiing. In

1992

the moguls event, competitors ski a run that is tightly packed with snow humps called moguls. Besides navigating the obstacle course cleanly, racers have to perform two airborne, or aerial, maneuvers. Weinbrecht grew up in New Jersey and taught herself the bumpy art of mogul skiing during the winter of 1985 in Vermont. At Albertville, racing in a snowstorm to the musical accompaniment of the Ramones' "Rock 'n' Roll High School," she narrowly beat Russian Yelizaveta Kozhevnikova for first place.

Duckpin History Rolls On

A Baltimore-born pastime slightly less well known than baseball (see the story on page 29) celebrated a new icon in 1992. On May 5, Pete Signore Jr. of North Haven, Connecticut, set a new world duckpin record by rolling a 279.

Duckpin is a century-old form of bowling that originated at Diamond Alleys in Baltimore—which happened to be owned by Wilbert Robinson and John J. McGraw, both of whom played for baseball's Baltimore Orioles in the early 1900s (they went on to become Hall of Fame managers with the Brooklyn Dodgers and New York Giants, respectively). Duckpins are sawed-off versions of traditional bowling pins. When the owners saw the way the small pins flew wildly around the alley, one of them remarked that it looked liked a "flock of flying ducks."

Duckpin bowlers use smaller balls (between five and six inches in diameter, versus the standard 8.59-inch bowling ball) and are allowed to roll three balls per turn. Played only in a handful of states, including Maryland, Connecticut, Indiana, and Massachusetts, duckpin and its enthusiasts have yet to bowl the elusive perfect 300 game.

Better Laettner than Never

In what many college basketball observers called the greatest game ever played, on March 28 the Duke University Blue Devils squeaked past the University of Kentucky Wildcats in the East Regional final of the men's NCAA tournament, 103–102. The one-point difference came in the closing 2.1 seconds of double overtime at the Spectrum in Philadelphia, when Duke's Christian Laettner snatched a long in-bounds pass from Grant Hill and nailed a miraculous 17-foot shot. The win sent the Blue Devils back to the Final Four in Minneapolis, where they went on to become the first repeat national champions in 19 years by handily defeating the University of Michigan in the final game, 71–51.

Laettner's magic moment at the Spectrum capped two and a half hours of classic basketball from the tournament's two best teams. They combined to make a phenomenal 61 percent of their shots. Still, all the precision passing, deft dribbling, and sharp shooting boiled down to the last two nail-biting possessions. After the Wildcats' Sean Woods banked in an off-balance running shot for the lead with 2.5 seconds remaining, it looked as if coach Rick Pitino's Kentucky team would be heading for the finals. But Laettner had other ideas.

The Blue Devils' center had already registered a perfect offensive performance. He was nine for nine from the field and 10 for 10 from the free-throw line. Plus, he was no stranger to fantastic finishes in the tournament: in 1990, he helped break the University of Connecticut's hearts with an overtime buzzer-beater that propelled Duke to the Final Four. Against Kentucky, Laettner caught Hill's pass with his back to basket, dribbled once, spun around, stopped, and popped—swish!

Everything Old Is New Again

On April 6, the Baltimore Orioles took baseball back to the future. Hosting the season's home opener, the team christened its new ballpark, Oriole Park at Camden Yards. Besides generating rave reviews and sold-out crowds, the stadium became the prototype for a new generation of "retro" venues around Major League Baseball.

Camden Yards, constructed on 85-acres at a cost of $110 million, has state-of-the-art scoreboards, grandstands, concessions, clubhouses, and other amenities. Yet it is designed in the style of charming, turn-of-the-20th-century, downtown ballparks that were integral centers of their communities. Steel, rather than concrete trusses, an arched brick facade, a sun roof over the sloped upper deck, an asymmetrical playing field, and a natural grass field are some of the nostalgic niceties.

Ebbets Field (Brooklyn Dodgers), Fenway Park (Boston Red Sox), Crosley Field (Cincinnati Reds), Wrigley Field (Chicago Cubs), and the Polo Grounds (New York Giants) were among the ballparks that served as powerful influences in the design of Oriole Park. Other retro parks that followed Camden Yards' lead over the next decade were Jacobs Field

Magic Moment *Co-captain Earvin "Magic" Johnson celebrates the U.S. men's basketball team's gold medal at the Olympics. NBA players were allowed to compete in the Games for the first time.*

(Cleveland Indians), Comerica Park (Detroit Tigers), Safeco Field (Seattle Mariners), Minute Maid Field (Houston Astros), SBC Park (San Francisco Giants), and Great American Ballpark (Reds).

The Dream Team

Barcelona, Spain, hosted the 1992 Summer Games, July 24 to August 9, with 9,370 of the world's best athletes

1992

competing in 257 events. A total of 169 nations competed. They included South Africa, which had been banned since 1960 for its apartheid policy, but had finally abandoned its racist social structure. A single German team appeared for the first time since Word War II, following the tearing down of the Berlin Wall. And there was a Unified Team comprising several former republics of the Soviet Union, which had collapsed in 1991.

This was the last year both the Winter and Summer Olympic Games were held in the same year, as they had been since the modern Olympics began in 1896. After 1992, the games were switched to a staggered schedule. The next Winter Games were held just two years later, in Lillehammer, Norway, and thereafter every four years. The next Summer Games were held four years later in Atlanta, Georgia.

For the first time, the International Olympic Committee opened men's basketball to professional players instead of only amateurs. USA Basketball, the governing body for hoops in the United States, responded by forming the Dream Team. Coached by the Detroit Pistons' Chuck Daly and co-captained by Magic Johnson and Larry Bird (b.1956), the team

also starred Charles Barkley (b.1963), Clyde Drexler, Patrick Ewing (b.1962), Michael Jordan, Karl Malone (b.1963), Chris Mullin, Scottie Pippen, David Robinson (b.1965), John Stockton (b.1962), and Duke University's Christian Laettner (see page 28).

The presence of Johnson, who had retired from the NBA the previous year after announcing that he was HIV-positive (see page 24), was a boost for people everywhere suffering from the dread disease. The fact that Johnson was still healthy and on his game, and that he still had legions of fans worldwide, did much to lift the sprits of those who had felt shunned and hopeless.

Arguably the greatest basketball team ever assembled, the Dream Team was criticized as being a grandiose display of pampered millionaires—a team that exemplified the big-business and mega-marketing elements that enveloped sports during the 1990s. (Coincidentally, NBA Commissioner David Stern was named 1992's most powerful man in sports in *The Sporting News'* annual top 100 listing.) The fact that the team elected to stay in a $900-a-night luxury hotel rather than the more modest Olympic Village with the rest of the world's athletes only fueled the fire. Four members of the team failed to show up for the Opening Ceremony. "It's very much like traveling with 12 rock stars," Daly remarked.

Wrote Tom Callahan of *U.S. News & World Report* in his post-Games analysis, "At the Olympic Games, where the truest dreamers have been swallowed up by a sensation, the Dream Team represents reality as much as anything else, although

Olympic Language

President George H.W. Bush, addressing a White House post-Games reception for the 1992 American Olympic Team, said, "I've watched so much Olympics that when [First Lady Barbara Bush] asked me to move a piece of furniture, I asked her, 'What's the degree of difficulty?'"

Dan and Dave and Dollars

Commercialism at the 1992 Olympics wasn't confined to basketball players. A couple of decathletes made financial headlines, too. Reebok International, a maker of sneakers and other sports apparel, signed Dan O'Brien (b.1966) and Dave Johnson to star in a $25 million advertising campaign, which humorously followed their rivalry to qualify for the U.S. Olympic Team. Dan was the reigning world champion in the 10-part, two-day decathlon; Dave held the record for the highest second-day score. One seemed destined to emerge as the world's greatest athlete.

At the qualifying meet for Olympics, however, Dan failed in the pole vault event and didn't make the team—thus suddenly canceling the Dan and Dave rivalry. Dave settled for the bronze medal in Barcelona, while Reebok was forced to revamp its ads. Undaunted, Dan set a new world record a month later at a meet in France.

it also represents Reebok, Nike, and the United States. Commercialism and professionalism have attended the games for decades—for centuries, truth to tell—but never before have they carried the flag or the day, and the reality is a sensation."

To no one's surprise, the Dream Team dazzled. They went undefeated in eight basketball games, scored more than 100 points in every one, and averaged a record-setting 117.25 points per game. They never called a timeout. The average margin of victory was 43.75 points, and the closest contest was over Croatia, 117–85, for the gold medal.

Jackie of All Trades

It's easy to see why Jackie Joyner-Kersee is considered by many to be the greatest female athlete ever. Just check out her trophy case. Hanging front and center are six Olympic medals, two of them golds won back to back at the 1988 and 1992 Summer Games in the grueling seven-event, two-day heptathlon, and another gold for the long jump in 1988.

There are trophies, medals, and newspaper clippings from her days as an All-America basketball star at the University of California at Los Angeles (UCLA), and when she was a three-sport standout at her hometown high school in East St. Louis, Illinois. What makes Joyner-Kersee's accomplishments even more impressive is that the multi-sport star has asthma.

Born on March 3, 1962, she was named after then President John F. Kennedy's wife, Jacqueline. "If you had asthma, they said you couldn't run or do some of the other things I was doing," said Joyner-Kersee, recalling when she was diagnosed with the disease at age 18. Undeterred, she went on to become the first lady of track and field in the United States, making her first Olympic team in 1984 and earning a silver medal in the heptathlon at the Los Angeles Games that year.

Joyner-Kersee (she married her UCLA track coach, Bob Kersee, in 1986) dominated the event for the next four years, winning all nine heptathlons she

1992

entered. The first woman to break the 7,000-point mark, she set world records twice again before eclipsing them all, scoring 7,291 points at the 1988 Games in Seoul, South Korea. She finished her Olympic career at the 1996 Games in Atlanta, where she took the bronze in the long jump.

Joyner-Kersee retired from competition in 1998. A year later, she was named one of the top six U.S. Olympians by *Sports Illustrated*, as well as the outstanding female Olympian of the century by a six-member panel of experts assembled by the Associated Press. She had left the sporting world breathless.

King Richard Abdicates

It promised to be a regal farewell. Instead, the last NASCAR (National Association for Stock Car Automobile Racing) Winston Cup race for Richard Petty (b.1937) went up in a ball of flames. On November 15 at Atlanta Motor Speedway, the winningest driver in NASCAR history lined up his famous No. 43 Pontiac alongside a field of competitors one

Other Milestones of 1992

✔ On April 8, tennis star Arthur Ashe (1943–1993) revealed that since 1988 he had been HIV-positive and that he now had AIDS.

✔ The University of Arkansas won its ninth consecutive NCAA men's indoor track and field championship on May 14.

✔ In the NBA Finals, the Chicago Bulls took two of three games in Portland against the Trailblazers, then rallied at home in game six on June 14 and became repeat champions.

✔ On May 11, the Naismith Memorial Basketball Hall of Fame inducted its first two women: Nera White, who from 1955 to 1969 led a team sponsored by the Nashville Business College to 10 Amateur Athletic Union national cham-

Dave Winfield

pionships, and Lucia Harris-Stewart, a member of the first U.S. Olympic women's basketball team in 1976.

✔ The NBA's Larry Bird retired on August 18. In 13 seasons, all with the Boston Celtics, he made 10 All-Star teams and won three MVP awards.

✔ On September 20, Philadelphia Phillies second baseman Mickey Morandini turned the first unassisted triple play in baseball's National League since May 30, 1927, in a 13-inning, 3–2 loss to the Pirates in Pittsburgh.

✔ In game six of the World Series, on October 24, Dave Winfield's two-out, two-run double in the 11th inning gave the Toronto Blue Jays a 4–3 lead and, ultimately, the championship, over the Atlanta Braves.

more time. The Hooters 500 was the final race of the NASCAR season and the last stop on his 29-race Fan Appreciation Tour, which he had announced the previous October.

The King, as stock car racing's most popular and successful driver had become known, was hanging up his crown (actually, a black cowboy hat, along with dark sunglasses) after a remarkable driving career that spanned 35 years. Petty began racing in 1958 for his legendary father, Lee Petty (1912–2000), one of NASCAR's pioneers and a three-time national champ. But the son eventually eclipsed his father. He had a record 200 career victories (second is David Pearson with 105); seven Winston Cup championships; seven Daytona 500 victories; Winston Cup Series Rookie of the Year honors (1959); and wins in 27 of 48 races in a single season (1967), including 10 in a row.

But Petty finished 35th in the Hooters 500 after getting tangled up in a fiery crash with Dick Trickle, Ken Schrader, and Darrell Waltrip. Still, the fans witnessed a great race. At the start, six drivers had a chance to earn enough points to win the season's Winston Cup Championship. It came down to Bill Elliott and Alan Kulwicki. Elliott won the race, but Kulwicki's second-place was enough to capture the year's title (the season championship, determined by finishes in

Long Live the King *As colorful as he was successful, Richard Petty retired from active NASCAR competition with a host of awards and a legion of fans.*

a year's worth of races) by a scant 10 points—the narrowest margin in NASCAR history.

The same day the King bade farewell, a young prince emerged. Finishing 31st in his first Winston Cup event was rookie Jeff Gordon (b.1971). Before the decade was out, Gordon captured three Cup titles and lead the series in wins five consecutive years (1995–1999). NASCAR racing had found a new member of its "royal" family.

1993

The Reich Stuff

"Wild" is one of two words that perfectly describe the NFL's AFC wild-card playoff game on January 3. The other is "greatest," as in greatest comeback in NFL history: The hometown Bills (11–5), hosting the Houston Oilers (10–6) at Rich Stadium in Buffalo, overcame a 32-point deficit to win in overtime, 41–38.

The two teams had squared off just a week earlier in the last game of the regular season, and the Oilers humiliated the Bills, 27–3. So by halftime in the playoff game, when the Oilers went comfortably into the locker room with a 28–3 lead, it looked like a repeat blowout. Instead, Houston simply blew it.

Buffalo quarterback Frank Reich, filling in for injured starter Jim Kelly, caught fire in the second half. After Houston intercepted a Reich pass and scored yet again, going up 35–3 early in the third quarter, Reich engineered six straight scoring drives—completing 16 of 23 passes for 230 yards and four touchdowns.

Reich was no stranger to comebacks. He's the guy who led the University of Maryland back from a 31–0 halftime deficit against the University of Miami in 1984 to a 42–40 victory—the greatest comeback in college football history.

When the Bills took the lead, 38–35, late in the fourth quarter, their fans were as delirious as the Oilers were dazed. Houston tied the game in the closing moments of regulation time, but in overtime the Bills intercepted a Warren Moon (b.1956) pass, which set up Steve Christie's 32-yard, game-winning field goal.

It was all for naught, though, as the Bills lost their third straight Super Bowl later in January.

He Courted Greatness

On February 6, Arthur Ashe died of AIDS at age 49. Ashe was the first male African-American tennis player to win the U.S. Open (1968) and Wimbledon (1975), and the first to play in the Davis Cup (1963). He was also a tireless champion for numerous social causes. He was outspoken about racism—including apartheid in South Africa—healthcare, education, and politics.

Born in Richmond, Virginia, on July 10, 1943, Ashe attended UCLA on a tennis scholarship and captured the NCAA

A Difficult Loss *Sports fans and non-sports fans mourned the death of Arthur Ashe, a pioneer on and off the court.*

singles title in 1965. He won 33 tournament victories from 1968 to 1979, and for 13 consecutive years ranked among the top five players in the world.

Ashe had a heart attack in 1979, which eventually forced his retirement from tennis in 1980. He soon embarked upon a career as an activist, youth tennis instructor, author, businessman, and television commentator. Ashe was elected to the International Tennis Hall of Fame in 1985.

His weakened heart required bypass surgery in 1983. From a blood transfu-

sions at the time, it is believed Ashe contracted the virus that causes AIDS. He chose not to reveal his condition until 1992, and only then because he believed that *USA Today* was about to report it. He dedicated the remainder of his life to AIDS education.

Following Ashe's death, Kenny Moore wrote in *Sports Illustrated*, "Ashe was of a time when the core of the American athlete was a sense of fair play. He believed he had control of his own behavior and therefore responsibility for his character."

The Filthy (Rich) Four

Chris Webber may have come up short in back-to-back NCAA finals, but he loomed large in the 1993 NBA draft on June 30. In fact, he led a fabulous foursome of underclassmen who were the first four picks. After the Orlando Magic took the 6-foot-10 Webber with the first pick, the Philadelphia 76ers chose Brigham Young University's 7-foot-6 center Shawn Bradley, the Golden State Warriors picked 6-foot-7 Memphis State guard Anfernee "Penny" Hardaway, and the Dallas Mavericks landed the University of Kentucky's Jamal Mashburn, a 6-foot-8 forward.

Indicative of the trend in signing young athletes to long-term contracts, these college kids became professional multimillionaires before ever starting an NBA game. Orlando traded Webber to Golden State for Hardaway and future picks on draft day; Webber signed with the Warriors for 15 years and $74.4 million; while Orlando gave Hardaway $65 million over 13 years. The 76ers inked Bradley to an eight-year, $44.28 million deal, and Mashburn got $32 million over seven years from Dallas. Timing, once again, was everything.

No Time-Out Like the Present

On April 5 in the New Orleans Superdome, with 20 seconds remaining in the NCAA men's basketball tournament final and the University of North Carolina clinging to a 73–71 lead, All-America forward Chris Webber of the University of Michigan rebounded a missed free throw, dribbled down the court, and called for a time-out. Except the Michigan Wolverines were out of time-outs — and now out of luck. Michigan was assessed a two-shot technical foul and Carolina went on to win, 77–71.

Webber's mistake not only effectively ended the game, but also the run of Michigan's fabled Fab Five. A year earlier, Webber headlined a quintet of highly touted freshman. He and Juwan Howard, Jalen Rose, Ray Jackson, and Jimmy King lived up to the hype and reached the 1992 finals, only to lose to a more experienced Duke University team. The preseason favorites in the 1992–93 college season, Michigan finished its regular schedule ranked third in the nation, with a 26–4 record and a number-one seed in the NCAA tournament.

It took a pair of overtime wins, against UCLA and the University of Kentucky, but the Fab Five advanced to the finals with UNC coach Dean Smith's (b.1931) 28–4 Tar Heels. It was Webber's final collegiate game. A month later he announced that he would enter the NBA draft (see the box above). This time, his timing was right: He was the number-one pick.

Swoopes Scoops Women's Hoops

"If Michael Jordan has a clone, it's Sheryl Swoopes." Those lofty words of praise were spoken on April 2 by Vanderbilt University women's basketball coach Jim Foster — and for good reason. Swoopes had just blistered his top-ranked Commodores for 31 points in leading the

Texas Tech Lady Red Raiders to a 60–46 victory in the semifinals of the 1993 NCAA women's Final Four.

In true Jordan-esque fashion, two nights later in the championship game against Ohio State, Swoopes scored more points than the entire Vanderbilt team, racking up 47 points in an 84–82 thriller. Swoopes tallied the most points that any player, male or female, ever managed in an NCAA final.

"When it was over, my first thought was, 'Is this real?'" she said in a post-game interview with the *Washington Post*. "At times, I get it in my mind that there is no way I can miss." Swoopes, a senior, became the second woman ever drafted by the all-male U.S. Basketball League. Selected by the Daytona Beach Hooters, she opted to go to Europe, where she played 10 games in an Italian league. In 1997, Swoopes joined the Women's National Basketball Association's Houston Comets, where she continued her winning ways.

Jordan Takes the Air Out of Basketball

In retrospect, the 1992–93 NBA season might have seemed routine to the guy who had to scale the rafters of Chicago Stadium to hang another banner. Or to whomever made the trophy for the league's leading scorer. Yet the road to the Chicago Bulls' third consecutive championship and Michael Jordan's seventh straight scoring title was anything but routine.

Collectively, the Bulls didn't have much trouble capturing the Central Division title again, with a 57–25 record, although they lost the coveted home-court advantage throughout the playoffs to the New York Knicks, who finished 60–22. Jordan, meanwhile, had to deal with the intense media scrutiny that grew from

One-Woman Show *Sheryl Swoopes (center) was an unstoppable force in the NCAA title game, scoring 47 points in Texas Tech's win.*

1993

published reports of his gambling excesses and late-night forays.

The Bulls swept the Atlanta Hawks and the Cleveland Cavaliers in the first two rounds of the playoffs in May, then had their hands full with coach Pat Riley's (b.1945) tough Knicks squad. Led by center Patrick Ewing (b.1962) and the league's best defense, New York won the first two games at home. The Bulls answered right back and took two in Chicago, with Jordan scoring 54 points in game four. In the pivotal game five back in New York's Madison Square Garden, an infamous closing-moments sequence—in which Knicks forward Charles Smith missed several point-blank chances to win the game—saved the Bulls' season.

The 4–2 series victory catapulted Chicago back into the NBA Finals, where the Bulls met the Phoenix Suns in June. Behind newly acquired Charles Barkley and sharp-shooters Danny Ainge and Dan Majerle, the Suns had gone 62–20, giving them homecourt advantage. But Jordan and the Bulls reversed that fortune by winning the first two games in Phoenix. The Suns prevailed in an epic, triple-overtime marathon in game three, but couldn't withstand Jordan's 55-point outburst in game four and eventually succumbed in six games. "Winning this championship was harder than anything I've done before in basketball," Jordan said.

His off-the-court life was about to become incredibly harder. On July 23, his beloved father—whom he often called his best friend—was murdered in North Carolina. Three months later, on October 6, still grief-stricken and increasingly disenchanted with the life of a public megas-

tar, Jordan shocked the sports world by announcing his retirement. At age 30 and with nine years of history-making basketball behind him, he called it quits—for the first time, but certainly not the last—while still at the top of his over-the-top game.

"I feel that at this particular time in my career I have reached the pinnacle of my career," Jordan said in his 1993 retirement press conference. "I have achieved a lot in that short amount of time, but I just feel I don't have anything else for myself to prove."

Krone's Ecstasy and Agony

Julie Krone (b.1963) hopped on a pony for the first time when she was five and galloped off from there to become the winningest female jockey in horse racing history. The highlight of her career came on June 5 at the 125th running of the Belmont Stakes in Belmont, New York. Aboard Colonial Affair, Krone became the first woman to ride a winner in a Triple Crown race. She had raced hundreds of times at the famous mile-and-a-half track, including three other Belmont Stakes, so she was familiar with the venue. This time, it counted the most. "I turned for home and told myself, Now I'm going to win the Belmont Stakes," she said afterward.

In late August, Krone made news again, though this time it was bad. Racing at Saratoga, she had an accident and badly shattered her right ankle. But she recovered and continued her remarkable racing career, retiring in 1999 with 3,545 wins, her mounts earning more than $81 million. A year later, she became the first

Tall in the Saddle

When he retired from baseball at the end of the 1993 season, Lynn Nolan Ryan, Jr. was 46 years old and still pitching 95 miles per hour. After pitching in the major leagues for 27 years, the gentleman rancher born on January 31, 1947, in Refugio, Texas, rode into the sunset holding more than 50 records, including most no-hitters (seven), most career strikeouts (5,714), and most strikeouts in a season (383 in 1973). Throwing heat over four decades for four teams (the New York Mets, California Angels, Houston Astros, and Texas Rangers), Ryan retired with 324 wins against 292 losses. He started more games (773) than anyone except Cy Young (815). He never won a Cy Young Award, but was inducted into the Baseball Hall of Fame in 1999.

In the May 1993 issue of *Texas Monthly* magazine, Joe Nick Petoski wrote a piece entitled "A Farewell to Arm," a sort of open letter to Ryan. Petoski's prose summed up Ryan, not so much in baseball terms, but in what he meant to the game, those who love it, and the state of Texas.

"I thought I would drop you this thank-you note—not so much for all the records you've shattered and all the milestones you've reached; not for all you've done for baseball in Texas, bringing excitement to the Astros a few years back and respectability to the Rangers today; not for being a walking, talking advertisement for the benefits of rigorous training and clean living; and certainly not for being a celebrity so

inextricably tied to our state that two roads—one in Arlington, between Houston and Freeport, near your hometown of Alvin—have been named the Nolan Ryan Expressway. The real reason I wanted to thank you was for being my seven-year-old's first hero. I couldn't have asked for a better role model. It's not just that you are a 46-year-old adult who plays a kid's game for a living, excelling in all aspects of your position— though that would be more than enough. You married your high school sweetheart. You raised your family in

Nolan Ryan

the same town in which you grew up. You're a cattleman—what could be more Texan? And rarely is heard a disparaging word about you. Years from now you may be exposed as a crank and a whiner, a showboat with a big head, or just another money-grubbing jock. But I'm not betting on it. From where I sit in the grandstand, you appear to be a class act, the last in a long line of good guys who seem to have vanished from your profession."

1993

woman inducted into the National Thoroughbred Racing Hall of Fame.

"I wish I could put every one of you here on a race horse at the eighth pole, so you could have the same feeling that I did," Krone said at the ceremony in Saratoga Springs, New York. "I got to do something I love so much every day. And today I know for sure that life doesn't get any better."

The Rarest of No-Hitters

Since St. Louis Brown Stockings righthander George "Grin" Bradley became the first Major League Baseball pitcher to do it, on July 15, 1876, pitching a no-hit baseball game has remained a remarkable personal achievement. But as hard as it is to pitch a complete game with no hits, they're not all that uncommon. At least one no-hitter has been thrown in all but three major league seasons (1982, 1989, 2000) since 1960. But the 2–0 no-hitter pitched on September 4, 1993, at Yankee Stadium by New York Yankees lefthander Jim Abbott is the only one of its kind.

It's not because Abbott shut down an explosive Cleveland Indians' lineup, featuring such All-Star hitters as Kenny Lofton, Albert Belle, Manny Ramirez, and Jim Thome—who just six days earlier had pounded him for 10 hits and seven runs in an inning and a third. Or because he struck out only three hitters but walked five, and each time wriggled out of trouble. It's because he has only one hand.

His entire life, Abbott had said "no" to accepting pity or being treated differently because he was born without a right hand. And he wouldn't take no for an answer when challenged to prove he

belonged on the pitcher's mound. At age 11, in his Little League pitching debut, he threw a no-hitter. He pitched the gold-medal-winning game against Japan in the 1988 Olympics. And without a day in the minor leagues, he jumped directly from the University of Michigan to the California Angels' starting rotation.

"I don't think I'm handicapped," Abbott told *Sports Illustrated for Kids* in 1994. "My hand hasn't kept me from doing anything I wanted to do. I believe you can do anything you want, if you put your mind to it."

Ryding High in England

Golf challenges an individual's physical and mental skills. It's each golfer for himself or herself up and down the fairways and putting greens. But every two years, the top American professional male golfers team up to compete against Europe's best pros in the Ryder Cup. There are no money prizes for the winners, only national pride and transatlantic bragging rights. So when the U.S. team rallied on the last day of the 1993 Ryder Cup—contested at The Belfry in Sutton Coldfield, England, September 24 to 26—the Stars and Stripes unfurled proudly.

Golf is considered a gentlemanly sport, with strictly enforced rules of play and etiquette. There's no trash talking between opponents. Things got a bit testy two years earlier, however, when the matches were held at Kiawah Island in South Carolina (the site alternates between the United States and Europe). Tensions ran high, with the post-Desert Storm Americans feeling patriotic (they donned camouflage caps one day),

Other Milestones of 1993

✔ On February 3, cantankerous Cincinnati Reds owner Marge Schott was suspended from baseball for one year and fined $25,000 for making derogatory racial and ethnic remarks.

✔ President Bill Clinton issued Proclamation 6527, declaring February 4 National Women and Girls in Sports Day. The proclamation recognized the achievements of women in the field of sports and their efforts to break down sexual and racial barriers.

Don Shula

✔ Major League Baseball welcomed two new teams, the Florida Marlins and the Colorado Rockies, on April 5.

✔ On September 7, St. Louis Cardinals outfielder Mark Whiten became the 12th Major League Baseball player to hit four home runs in a single game.

✔ Miami Dolphins head coach Don Shula won his NFL-record 325th game with a 19–14 victory over the Philadelphia Eagles in Philadelphia on November 14.

European charges of cheating, and other back-and-forth head games.

Now, the competition at The Belfry boiled down to the last day. The Americans trailed late in the competition, but Ryder Cup rookie Davis Love III pulled out a critical victory over Constantino Rocca, and the U.S. team won 15-13. America got the Cup back for the first time since 1983. Graciously, both teams accepted the outcome.

Carter and Blue Jays Walk Off with Another Title

On October 23, Joe Carter (b.1960) strode to home plate in the bottom of the ninth inning. Pressure? It was only game six of the World Series, with Carter's Toronto Blue Jays up three games to two over the Philadelphia Phillies. The Jays were losing, 6–5, at the Skydome in Toronto. The veteran outfielder stood in

against the Phillies' hard-throwing closing pitcher, Mitch Williams, who had recorded a career-high 43 saves during the regular season.

But "the Wild Thing" had been living up to his wicked-fastball-shaky-control nickname in the series, saving game two, then blowing game four. On this day, Williams walked Rickey Henderson to lead off the ninth inning, induced a fly out, then gave up a single to Paul Molitor (b.1956). Carter worked the count to 2–2 as the raucous Skydome crowd urged him on. Williams wound up, delivered…and so did Carter, sending the ball over the leftfield fence. The Blue Jays won, 8–6!

Toronto thus became the first team to win back-to-back World Series since the New York Yankees in 1977–78. More incredible was Carter's walk-off homer, only the second ever to end a Series, and the first come-from-behind Series winner.

1994

Seminoles Win Two Close Ones

The New Year started out doubly nice for Florida State University's football team. First, the Seminoles pulled out a dramatic, 18–16 victory over the University of Nebraska in the Orange Bowl in Miami on January 1. Then, a day later, the team was voted national champions for the first time in school history.

Florida State won its game when freshman Scott Bentley kicked a 22-yard field goal with 24 seconds left, and Nebraska's Byron Bennett misfired on a 45-yard try as time ran out. The Fighting Irish of the University of Notre Dame also won on New Year's Day, edging Texas A&M University, 24–21, in the Cotton Bowl. What's more, back on November 13, Notre Dame had beaten Florida State. The Irish finished the season with a 11–1 record, Florida State with a 12–1 record. On the strength of their head-to-head win, Notre Dame head coach Lou Holtz (b.1937) complained that the Irish should have been ranked number one.

So it goes in the always-spinning world of sports debates. This one will probably rage forever.

Super Bowl XXVII: 2–0 vs. 0–4

There are winners and there are losers. And somewhere in between are the Buffalo Bills. Remarkably, they reached the Super Bowl for an unprecedented fourth year in a row. More incredibly, with a 30–13 rout at the hands of the Dallas Cowboys on January 30 at the Georgia Dome in Atlanta, the Bills lost their fourth Super Bowl in a row—also unprecedented.

While Buffalo was left to ponder their triumphs and tragedies, Dallas hoisted the Lombardi Trophy for the second straight year. The Cowboys had whipped these same Bills in Super Bowl XXVI, 52–17. Dallas now joined the Green Bay Packers, Miami Dolphins, Pittsburgh Steelers (who did it twice), and San Francisco 49ers as the only teams to win back-to-back Super Bowls.

The rematch favored the Cowboys. Despite losing their first two regular-season games and overcoming injuries to quarterback Troy Aikman (b.1966) and running back Emmitt Smith (b.1969), the Cowboys went 12–4 to win the NFC East. They sailed through the playoffs, dis-

Man on the Run *Accused murderer O.J. Simpson took to the road in his white Ford Bronco (page 46).*

pensing the Packers and the 49ers. Buffalo finished 12–4 as well to capture the AFC East, then beat the Los Angeles Raiders and the Kansas City Chiefs in the playoffs. Still, they were considered the underdogs against the reigning NFL champs.

The Bills led at halftime, 13–6, but fell apart from there under the Cowboys' speedy, powerful defense and their massive offensive line. Buffalo turned the ball over three times, including a costly third-quarter fumble by runningback Thurman Thomas that was returned 46 yards for a touchdown. Smith, on the merit of his 132 rushing yards and two touchdowns, was named the game's MVP.

Winter Wonderland

The XXVII Olympic Winter Games were held in idyllic Lillehammer, Norway, February 12 to 27. The friendly, well-organized venue and outstanding

1994

athletic achievements combined for one of the most successful Olympics ever. The United States brought home 13 medals—six gold, five silver, and two bronze—while host Norway doubled that total to win the most medals at the Games.

Although the women's figure skating competition generated the juiciest headlines (see page 45), the speed skating events best epitomized the genuine Olympic spirit. Norway's own Johann Koss wowed the home crowd by winning three golds—in the 1,500-meter, 5,000-meter, and 10,000-meter races. American skater Bonnie Blair took her third straight Olympic title in the 500-meter sprint and second straight in the 1,000-meter race. Her trove of five gold medals, dating back to the 1988 Calgary Games, are the most won by an American female athlete in either summer or winter.

Unlike Blair, Dan Jansen (b.1965) appeared to be cursed in Olympic competition. One of the greatest sprinters in speed skating history, he had won the world sprint championship twice, won seven overall World Cup titles, and set seven world records. Yet he failed to win any medal at the 1984 Olympics. Four years later, at the Winter Games in Calgary, Jansen was distraught over the death of his sister the day of the 500-meter final, and he slipped and fell during the race. The same thing happened in the 1,000-meter race.

Jansen finished out of the medals again at the 1992 Albertville Games. Unbelievably, he slipped in the 500-meter in Lillehammer and finished eighth. His last chance came in the 1,000-meter race.

Powered by what he would later describe in his autobiography, *Full Circle*, as "a jolt of energy" in his legs, Jansen not only finished in first place, but set a world record. With fans of every nation cheering, he skated a victory lap around the Viking Ship oval with his infant daughter, named after his late sister, Jane, in his arms— and a hard-earned gold medal around his neck.

A comparatively unknown American came out of nowhere to win the gold medal in the men's downhill skiing event. Tommy Moe, a skiing prodigy from Montana, had never even won a World Cup race before hitting the slopes in Lillehammer. Thirty thousand Norwegians watched in agony as Moe edged native son Kjetil Andre Aamodt by four one-hundredths of a second for the gold medal. The blow was later softened when it was learned that Moe's great-great grandfather was Norwegian.

Rangers End a 53-Year Freeze-Out

The New York Rangers won the Stanley Cup in 1940. Not until June 14 did they again possess the National Hockey League's championship trophy. No NHL team or fans had ever waited so long, and the Rangers ended their drought in thrilling fashion.

Haunted by its cursed past, the team began a serious rebuilding effort in 1991 by acquiring Mark Messier (b.1961), who had been captain of the Edmonton Oilers for five Stanley Cup titles. In April 1993, highly regarded Mike Keenan (b.1949) signed on to coach the team, which, by the start of the 1993–94 season, featured six members of Messier's championship-rich Oilers' squad. The Rangers compiled the league's best record during the regular season (52-24-8, with 112 points), then breezed through the first two rounds of the playoffs.

The going got tougher in the Eastern Conference finals against the New Jersey Devils, who went up three games to two in the best-of-seven series. That's when Messier proved his mettle, guaranteeing victory before game six and then going out and scoring three third-period goals in the Rangers' 4–2 win. Game seven proved to be a nail-biter, too, with New York prevailing in double overtime.

In the finals against the Vancouver Canucks, the Rangers lost game one, then won three straight. But after they lost the next two games, memories of frustrations past loomed. Messier came to the rescue again in game seven at home in Madison Square Garden, scoring the go-ahead goal. Up 3–2, New York survived a furious third-period attack by Vancouver before wildly celebrating the end of their Stanley Cup drought.

As the Skates Turn

You can't make this stuff up, unless perhaps for a sleazy soap-opera script. That's pretty much what the sordid Olympic tale of archrival figure skaters Tonya Harding and Nancy Kerrigan seemed like.

Scene 1: Our story opens just after Christmas 1993. Harding, her ex-husband, and two other shady characters conspire to attack and injure Kerrigan— the reigning U.S. champion, Olympic favorite, and thorn in Harding's side—to keep her from competing in the upcoming U.S. Skating Championships.

Scene 2: On January 6, following a practice session in Detroit, Kerrigan is clubbed on her right knee. The unknown attacker flees. Two days later, Harding wins the national title, from which the injured Kerrigan has had to withdraw. Kerrigan is named to the team anyway.

Scene 3: Several witnesses come forward and tip off FBI agents about the plot. Arrests follow, though Harding is spared. She denies any knowledge or involvement, until her ex-hubby cuts a deal with the Feds and squeals on her. Harding finally confesses that she knew he was involved, but found out only after the attack. She sues the U.S. Olympic Committee (USOC) to prevent it from kicking her off the Olympic team. The USOC blinks, and the Tonya and Nancy Show shifts to Norway.

Scene 4: Kerrigan leads after the short program, Harding is in 10th place, and CBS basks in the sixth highest-rated television broadcast of all time. On February 25, petite Ukranian teenager Oksana Baiul edges Kerrigan for the gold. On the medal stand, silver-medalist Kerrigan, unaware her microphone is on, makes snotty remarks about Baiul. Harding, who finished eighth, is nowhere to be found.

Epilogue: Kerrigan turns pro, gets involved with a married man, and skates in ice shows. Harding pleads guilty to conspiracy, is banned from competition, and, years later, clubs opponents as a celebrity boxer.

O.J. Runs
Out of Bounds

Orenthal James "O.J." Simpson (b.1947) was a marvel to watch on the football field. As an All-America running back for the University of Southern California, he won the 1968 Heisman Trophy. Over 11 seasons in the NFL (1969–1979), the first nine with the Buffalo Bills, he amassed 11,236 rushing yards—including a then-record 2,003 yards in 1973. He won the league's MVP award that year. When he retired from football, Simpson segued from football player to affable broadcaster, actor, and television pitchman.

On June 17, the nation marveled at TV images of O.J. on the run again, only this time in a white Ford Bronco being chased by the Los Angeles Police Department (LAPD). Simpson finally surrendered and was charged with the stabbing murders of his ex-wife Nicole Brown Simpson and her friend Ronald Goldman, whose bodies were found on June 12. From there unfolded one of the most sensational trials of the 20th century.

Simpson's criminal trial didn't begin until the following January. It lasted more than nine months, generating nearly round-the-clock media coverage and public debate. Even late-night comedians routinely tossed O.J. jokes into their monologues. The prosecution presented mounds of potentially incriminating testimony and physical evidence, none more dramatic than DNA that matched Simpson's blood to that found at the crime scene. His defense was built around accusations of a racially motivated frame-up by the LAPD. The jury, after less than four hours of deliberation, returned a not guilty verdict on October 3, 1995, and Simpson was released from prison.

Nearly three weeks later, Simpson went on trial in a separate civil case resulting from a lawsuit by the victims' families. On January 4, 1996, a jury concluded that he had wrongfully caused the deaths of his ex-wife and Goldman. The court ordered Simpson to pay compensatory damages of $8.5 million and punitive damages of $25 million.

The entire saga provided the public with a vivid portrayal of the justice system and of racial divisions in the country, as well as a glimpse into the future trend of reality television.

Meanwhile, the Knicks' Agony Continues

Unlike the New York Rangers, with whom they shared Madison Square Garden, the New York Knicks just missed their Garden party when they lost game seven of the NBA Finals to the Houston Rockets on June 22 at The Summit in Houston. It would have been the Knicks' first title since 1973.

Seven-foot centers Patrick Ewing of the Knicks and Hakeem Olajuwon were certainly the centers of attention in this rough-and-tumble defensive battle, in which neither team scored more than 93 points in any of the seven games. Even so, it was the play of guards Sam Cassell of Houston and John Starks of the Knicks that ultimately made the difference.

With the series tied at one game apiece, Cassell scored seven points in the final seconds of game three in New York to preserve a 93–89 Rockets win. The Knicks won the next two and hoped to finish things off in game six in Houston. Starks, pouring in 27 points, nearly made it happen. But he came up just short in two critical possessions in the closing moments, including a 25-footer blocked by Olajuwon with two seconds left and New York down 86–84.

Starks went ice cold in game seven—2 for 18, including 0 for 11 from three-point range. The Rockets won 90–84 and landed their first NBA championship.

The World Cup Runneth Over

 Imagine if Major League Baseball held the World Series in Britain.

America's national pastime in a country where the game of cricket is far more popular? It could never happen!

But when FIFA, the international organization that governs soccer, announced that the 1994 World Cup Tournament would be staged in the United States, skeptics wondered what it was thinking. Soccer's grandest event—so special that it is only held every four years—in a country where only little kids play the sport?

Well, not only did the U.S. host the 15th World Cup from June 17 to July 17, but it was also a huge success. Teams from 24 nations played a total of 52 games in arenas across the country, including Giants Stadium in East Rutherford, New Jersey, Soldier Field in Chicago, the Cotton Bowl in Dallas, and the Rose Bowl in Pasadena, California. Nearly 3.5 million fans turned out, while a television audience of more than 35 million tuned in.

Youth soccer is tremendously popular in the United States, and high school and college soccer are growing. Still, the U.S. national team has never been a powerhouse. It often recruits players from Europe and South America, where football—as soccer is called in most of the world—is the number one sport. So it was shocking when the United States upset title contender Colombia, 2–1, in the first round before a crowd of 93,194 at the Rose Bowl on June 22. Indeed, it was the first win in World Cup play for the United States since beating England in 1950.

The United States advanced to the Round of 16, where it was beaten by Brazil on July 4 at Stanford Stadium in Stanford, California. Brazil moved on to the finals against Italy on July 17 at the Rose Bowl. The game ended in a tie and had to be decided on a shootout, in which each team alternates in taking five individual shots against the goalie. Brazil won the shootout, 3–2, and the World Cup.

Baseball Strikes Out

By August, the Major League Baseball season was one of the most exciting fans had seen in a long time. Matt Williams, Ken Griffey Jr. (b.1969), and Frank Thomas (b.1968) were on home run tears, each threatening to break Roger Maris' single-season record of 61 homers set in 1961. Tony Gwynn (b.1960) was flirting with a .400 batting average, a mark

Flag Day *American soccer players whoop it up after a stunning upset of Colombia in the World Cup. It was the first U.S. victory in the tournament in 44 years.*

1994

that hadn't been hit since Ted Williams finished the 1941 season at .406. The New York Yankees, who last won a World Series in 1978, were in first place in the American League. The Montreal Expos, with a measly $18.5 million payroll, were atop the National League.

Just after midnight on August 12, it all came to a screeching halt. That's the day the players went on strike. As with the previous seven work stoppages, dating back to 1972 (four player strikes and three lockouts by team owners), the main issue was money. This time the owners wanted to institute a cap on salaries, limiting how much teams could spend on their total player payroll—something the players' union strongly opposed.

For the next 34 days, fans kept their fingers crossed that the two sides would come to an agreement and resume one of the best seasons in years. Instead, the unthinkable happened. On September 14, acting Commissioner Bud Selig announced that the remainder of the season was cancelled, including the playoffs and the World Series. The strike did not end until March 31, 1995. In those 232 days, 920 games were missed.

In a League of His Own

On September 5, the San Francisco 49ers' Jerry Rice left little doubt that he was the best wide receiver in the history of the NFL. In a 44–14 wipeout of the Los Angeles Raiders on the league's prime-time stage, *Monday Night Football*, he caught three touchdown passes. The last one established an NFL record, pushing him one touchdown past legendary Cleveland Browns fullback Jim Brown for a career total of 127—and still counting.

Jerry Lee Rice was born on October 13, 1962, in Crawford, Mississippi, where he became a high school star in football, basketball, and track. During four seasons at Mississippi Valley State University (1980–1984), Rice set 18 NCAA Division I-AA records. In his senior year alone, the consensus All-American racked up 1,845 yards and scored 28 touchdowns.

San Francisco head coach Bill Walsh scouted the 6-foot-2, 200-pound receiver and traded up for the 16th spot in the 1985 NFL draft specifically to land Rice.

San Francisco Treat *Prolific wide receiver Jerry Rice was still going strong in his 10th NFL season in 1994, when he became the NFL's all-time leading touchdown scorer.*

Other Milestones of 1994

✔ Wayne Gretzky of the Los Angeles Kings scored his 802nd career goal on March 23 to break Gordie Howe's all-time NHL scoring record.

✔ With a famous Arkansan, President Bill Clinton, in attendance at the Charlotte Coliseum in North Carolina, the University of Arkansas beat Duke, 76–72, to claim the NCAA basketball championship on April 4.

✔ Sprinter Leroy Burrell set a new world record (9.85 seconds) in the 100-meter sprint on July 6 in Lausanne, Switzerland.

✔ On July 28, Texas Rangers baseball pitcher Kenny Rogers threw a perfect game (no hits, no walks, no runs, and no players to reach first base), blanking the California Angels, 4–0.

✔ After rallying from six holes back, Tiger Woods, at age 18, became the youngest winner of the U.S. Amateur Golf Championship on August 28.

✔ On September 11, Andre Agassi beat Germany's Michael Stich in straight sets to become the first unseeded player to win the men's U.S. Open tennis title since 1966.

Andre Agassi

The rookie wide receiver scored his first touchdown on a 25-yard pass from quarterback Joe Montana on October 10, 1986, and he has just gotten better from there.

By the end of the 2003 season with the Raiders (he left the 49ers after 2000), the 41-year-old Rice had shattered virtually every receiving record there is, including receptions (1,519), receiving yards (22,466), touchdowns (194), most 1,000-yard receiving seasons (14), and most 100-catch seasons (4).

In three Super Bowl wins with the 49ers (XXIII, XXIV, and XXIX), he caught 28 passes for 512 yards and seven touchdowns. He earned the MVP trophy in San Francisco's 20–16 win over Cincinnati in Super Bowl XXIII with his 11-catch, 215-yard performance.

Tar Heels' Dynasty Sticks

The University of North Carolina's women's soccer team won its ninth straight NCAA title on November 20 in Portland, Oregon, shutting out Notre Dame, 5–0. When the North Carolina Tar Heels won their first title, in 1982, there were only 25 women's teams competing on the NCAA Division I level in soccer. In 1994 there were 154, including 24 in the tournament. That was certainly evidence of soccer's growth in the United States, but more so of UNC's utter dominance of the sport.

1995

49ers Mine More Super Bowl Gold

The San Francisco 49ers had been the NFL's team of the decade in the 1980s. Quarterback extraordinaire Joe Montana was the catalyst for four Super Bowls wins during that decade. But he now played quarterback for the Kansas City Chiefs, leaving Steve Young (b.1961) to fill some big shoes.

Montana had made a career of throwing the ball to All-Pro wide receiver Jerry Rice (see page 48), and Young-to-Rice certainly sounded strange. Yet it produced similarly spectacular results. The new tandem connected on 112 passes for 1,499 yards and 13 touchdowns during the regular season. And that was just a tune-up for Super Bowl XXIX on January 29 at Joe Robbie Stadium in Miami.

San Francisco's biggest postseason challenge was a Dallas Cowboys' team on a quest for its third straight NFL championship. The 49ers got past the Cowboys on November 13, and again two months later in the NFC Championship Game.

That matchup turned out to be the season's pivotal game because the Super Bowl was yet another NFC blowout. In whipping the San Diego Chargers, 49–26, the 49ers made it 11 AFC defeats in a row. It was the record fifth Super Bowl victory for the San Francisco franchise.

Young passed successfully to Rice 10 times for 149 yards and three touchdowns in the Super Bowl. Young finished the day with 24 completions in 36 attempts and a record six touchdowns. After the game, 49ers head coach George Seifert—who himself knew about replacing a legend after taking over for Bill Walsh in 1989—called Young one of the greatest quarterbacks in league history. "Joe Montana established a standard," he said, "and Steve Young has maintained it."

He's Ba-a-a-a-a-ack!

You're the best basketball player on the planet, so why quit to take up baseball? That question probably crossed Michael Jordan's mind during his 17-month hiatus from the NBA. So after a season of Minor League Baseball, the former outfielder rejoined the Chicago Bulls on March 19. In his first game back, against the Indiana Pacers—and wearing his baseball number 45 instead of his familiar 23—Jordan scored 19 points.

The Big Squeeze *San Francisco 49ers quarterback Steve Young hugs the Vince Lombardi Trophy after leading his team to victory in Super Bowl XXIX.*

If there was any rust on the 32-year-old Jordan's game, he shook it off against his old rival, the New York Knicks. On March 28, he set a Madison Square Garden record with 55 points in a 113–111 Bulls' squeaker. He looked pretty much his old self in leading Chicago to a first-round victory in the playoffs against the Charlotte Hornets, averaging 31.5 points in four games. Yet, despite Jordan's vintage

This Girl's Got Game *Forward Rebecca Lobo and the University of Connecticut soared to the NCAA women's basketball title with a 35-0 record. UConn vanquished University of Tennessee in the title game.*

Perfectly Done

The University of Connecticut's women's basketball team did more than win the NCAA Division I Championship on April 2, defeating the University of Tennessee, 70–64. They even did more than complete the season with a perfect 35–0 record. The Lady Huskies put women's college basketball on the map.

Not that women didn't already have game. Superstars such as Cheryl Miller and Sheryl Swoopes had paved the way at the University of Southern California and Texas Tech University, respectively. And Tennessee's Pat Summit, with 564 wins by season's end, was one of the nation's most accomplished head coaches, man or woman. This UConn squad, though, took the game to a new level.

The poster girl was Rebecca Lobo (b.1973), a 6-foot-4 forward with a great perimeter game and a 4.0 grade-point average—an amazing role model to legions of girls. She and the Huskies earned the number-one ranking in January after knocking off Tennessee, and they never looked back. In the title game, at the Target Center in Minneapolis, Lobo got into foul trouble in the first half, which helped Tennessee's Lady Vols to a 38–32 half-time advantage. Lobo and point guard Jennifer Rizzotti led the charge back, though, and UConn completed its dream season in perfect fashion.

They're Ba-a-a-a-ack!

Major League Baseball returned from its longest work stoppage on April 25. The shortened season—144

38-point effort in game two in the next round of the playoffs, against Shaquille O'Neal (b.1972) and the Orlando Magic, the Bulls lost the series, four games to two.

"We weren't the same team we were 18 months ago," Jordan admitted in the post-game press conference, "but the fun part is trying to live up to the accomplishments of the past."

games instead of the normal 162—produced enough goodwill to begin winning back the hearts of disgruntled fans. Bad teams did well, good players did better, and Cal Ripken simply did what no one else had done before (see page 54).

The Cleveland Indians, long the doormats of the American League, finished with 100 wins for the first time since 1954. The Seattle Mariners reached the postseason for the first time in team history. Their thrilling, extra-innings victory in game five of the division series in September against the New York Yankees, who hadn't won anything since 1981, lifted them to the American League Championship Series (ALCS). Although the Mariners fell to the Indians, who won the best-of-seven ALCS in six games, the run probably saved baseball in Seattle.

The Colorado Rockies, in just their third season, made the playoffs, but lost to the pitching-rich Atlanta Braves (ace Greg Maddux, thanks to a 19–2 record and a skimpy 1.63 ERA, won his unprecedented fourth straight Cy Young Award). The Braves then swept the Cincinnati Reds and faced the Indians in a World Series in October that confirmed the old saying that good pitching beats good hitting.

As a team, the Indians hit .291 for the season—the best in Major League Baseball. Their lineup featured Albert Belle, who rang up 50 home runs, and veteran Eddie Murray, who whacked his 3,000th career hit on June 30. The Braves' pitching staff had the lowest ERA, at 3.44, in the major leagues.

Maddux opened the Series with a two-hit gem in which he pitched all nine innings; only four balls left the infield.

Down two games to none, the Indians won two of three games at home. In game six back in Atlanta, Tom Glavine pitched eight innings and gave up just one hit, David Justice smacked a sixth-inning homer, and closing pitcher Mark Wohlers threw a perfect ninth inning to seal the 1–0 Braves' win. It marked the team's return to baseball's mountaintop after a 37-year absence—and baseball's return to the hearts of its fans.

Rockets-Powered Sweep

The Houston Rockets swept the Orlando Magic in four games to repeat as NBA champions. While some liked to believe their 1994 title had a lot to do with a Chicago Bulls team that no longer

The Nation Mourns

On April 23, audiences at sports arenas, stadiums, and ballparks across the country observed a moment of silence to honor the victims of what was then the worst terrorist attack ever in the United States. On the morning of April 19, a massive bomb hidden inside a rental truck exploded in front of the Murrah Federal Building in Oklahoma City, killing 168 men, women, and children. Just 90 minutes later, an Oklahoma Highway Patrol officer pulled over 27-year-old Timothy McVeigh for driving without a license plate. Shortly before he was to be released on April 21, McVeigh, an Army veteran, was recognized as a bombing suspect and was charged with the deadly crime. Not long after, an ex-Army friend, Terry Nichols, was also arrested and charged. The men were tried in two separate, emotional, and highly publicized trials. In June 1997, a jury convicted McVeigh and sentenced him to death. He was executed on June 11, 2001. Nichols was found guilty of involuntary manslaughter and of conspiring with McVeigh. He was sentenced to life in prison.

Baseball's New Iron Man

New York Yankees legend Lou Gehrig (1903–1941) earned the nickname "The Iron Horse" after playing in 2,130 consecutive games. That seemingly insurmountable record was eclipsed at Baltimore's Camden Yards on September 6 in what proved to be baseball's greatest welcome-back gift back to strike-weary fans. On that festive summer evening, Baltimore Orioles shortstop Cal Ripken Jr. (b.1960) played in his 2,131st straight game.

Once the fifth inning of the contest against the California Angels was complete and the game became official, Ripken ran a victory lap around the stadium, stopping and shaking hands with fans and players. The scoreboard read, "Cal, thank you for saving baseball." During a 22-minute, 15-second ovation, Ripken received eight curtain calls from the appreciative crowd.

"I know that if Lou Gehrig is looking down on tonight's activities," he told the throng, "he isn't concerned about someone playing one more consecutive game than he did. Instead, he's viewing tonight as just another example of what is good and right about the great American game."

Ripken began his iron man streak on May 30, 1982, and played in 19,231 out of a possible 19,395 innings. And he went all-out in every single one. Even in this most special of games, he homered to help boost the Orioles to a 4–2 win.

A local boy, born on August 24, 1960, in nearby Havre de Grace, Ripken earned AL Rookie of the Year honors in 1982 and was twice named the league's MVP (1983 and 1991). He started in 17 straight All-Star Games beginning in 1984 (the last three as a third baseman), and hit more home runs than any other short-stop (402).

At 6-foot-4, Ripken was the tallest full-time shortstop, and he set the single-season fielding percentage (a measure of defensive success calculated by dividing the number of successful plays a fielder makes by the total chances he has to play the ball) at the position (.996 in 1990). He recorded the final putout in the 1983 World Series, when the Orioles defeated the Philadelphia Phillies in five games for their first championship since 1970.

Ripken ended his streak at 2,632 games by taking himself out of the lineup on September 20, 1998. He retired at the end of the 2001 season with a lifetime batting average of .297 in 3,001 games. Next stop: the Baseball Hall of Fame.

Cal Ripken Jr.

had Michael Jordan, the Rockets put that notion to rest. In fact, after the 113–101 game four on June 14 in Houston, the Rockets became the first team in NBA history to defeat four 50-win teams on the way to a championship. Before sweeping the Magic, they put away, in order, the Utah Jazz, the Phoenix Suns, and the San Antonio Spurs. And in none of those series did the Rockets have home-court advantage.

X Marks the Sport

🏆 The amateur athletes of Generation X (those born between 1965 and 1975) explored new sporting thrills in the 1990s. Shunning tradition, they pioneered alternative sports such as inline skating, snowboarding, mountain biking, and street luge.

ESPN, the all-sports cable channel, quickly saw the potential and seized on a programming opportunity to appeal to a key audience by launching the Extreme Games. Held June 24 to July 1 in Rhode Island and Vermont, the inaugural games featured 27 events, including bungee jumping, barefoot waterski jumping, kite skiing, windsurfing, sky surfing, and bicycle stunt riding.

Not only was the competition gnarly, but it also proved a ratings hit with the all-important group of male TV viewers aged 12 to 34 that advertisers covet. So it was a no-brainer for ESPN to capitalize on the extreme theme every year.

ESPN added a winter version in 1996 and shortened the name to X Games. The snow and ice edition featured such extreme sports as snowboarding, ice climb-

ing, and super-modified shovel racing. Continued success and popularity eventually made the X Games a prime-time event for a new generation of international athletes and TV audiences for years to come.

NBC Locks Up the Olympics

⊙ Americans got their first look at the Olympics on television in 1960, when CBS paid the International Olympic Committee $50,000 to air 15 hours of the Winter Games from Squaw Valley, California.

X Marks the Spot *ESPN cornered a coveted demographic with the introduction of the Extreme Games. The X Games, as they soon were called, quickly grew in stature and popularity.*

1995

On August 7, 1995, NBC paid a whopping $1.25 billion for the U.S. rights to broadcast the 2000 Summer Games from Sydney, Australia, as well as the Winter Games from Salt Lake City, Utah, two years later.

Securing the television rights to sporting events had become a highly competitive business. Viewers never seemed to get enough sports—consider the popularity of cable channel ESPN—and advertisers wanted to reach those audiences. So the networks battled one another and paid millions to air baseball, football, and basketball. (As one example, on November 6, Major League Baseball announced a five-year, $1.7 billion deal with NBC, ESPN, Fox, and Prime Liberty Cable.)

The Olympics, now alternating every two years between Summer and Winter Games (see page 30), generated huge prime-time television ratings for two weeks. Although the networks didn't necessarily make money broadcasting them because the expenses involved in covering them were so high, they benefited from the prestige and the opportunity to promote their other programming.

ABC had dominated Olympics broadcasting through the 1980s, and NBC landing the Sydney and Salt Lake Games was considered a coup. The deal involved two rounds of international dealing by NBC Sports president Dick Ebersol. It began with a secret New York-to-Sweden-to-

Other Milestones of 1995

✔ On January 6, Atlanta Hawks head coach Lenny Wilkens notched career win No. 939—a 112–90 defeat of the Washington Bullets—to become the NBA's all-time winningest coach, surpassing the Boston Celtics' Red Auerbach.

✔ Sterling Marlin, on February 19, became the first NASCAR driver to win back-to-back Daytona 500s since Richard Petty repeated in 1974.

✔ Doug Swingley and his nine-dog team finished the Iditarod Trail Sled Dog race across Alaska on March 14 in record time, completing the 1,160-mile course in nine days, two hours, 42 minutes, 19 seconds.

Doug Swingley and team

✔ On June 24, the New Jersey Devils completed their four-game sweep of the Detroit Red Wings to win the NHL's Stanley Cup.

✔ By defeating German Boris Becker on July 9, Pete Sampras became the first U.S. male tennis player to win three consecutive Wimbledon championships.

✔ Dan Marino, quarterback of the Miami Dolphins, completed career pass number 3,687 in a 27–24 loss to the Indianapolis Colts to set an NFL record. He retired in 1999 also holding career records for completions, yards, and touchdowns.

Montreal-to-New York trip in early August, during which he outfoxed Fox Network owner Rupert Murdoch, who had offered the IOC $701 million for the Sydney rights. Ebersol upped the ante to $705 million, and in an unusual move, he got the Salt Lake Games for an extra $545 million—marking the first time the IOC had sold more than one Olympics at a time. Four months later, on December 12, in an even more-stunning move, NBC announced that it had secured the rights to every Summer and Winter Games through 2008 for an equally stunning $2.3 billion.

The Glass Slipper Fits Northwestern

Who knows how Cinderella came to be associated with sports teams? But there seems to be one or two Cinderella stories every year—teams relegated to the dust pile who unexpectedly outshine the competition. In 1995, the role fell to the Northwestern University Wildcats football team. For ages a perennial loser in the Big Ten Conference, Northwestern enjoyed one of those when-you-wish-upon-a-star seasons.

It started on September 2 in South Bend, Indiana, when the Wildcats stunned the Notre Dame Fighting Irish, 17–15. Northwestern, a 28-point underdog, had last beaten the Irish in 1962. On October 7, the Wildcats marched into Ann Arbor and upset the University of Michigan Wolverines, 19–13. A week later, they magically made the University of Wisconsin's Badgers disappear, 35–0! On November 4, the sixth-ranked Wildcats hosted number-12 Penn State University and tamed the Nittany Lions, 21–10. In that game, Northwestern running back Darnell Autry gained 100 yards in his 10th straight game, set a school season rushing record, and scored three touchdowns.

When Michigan spoiled previously unbeaten and second-ranked Ohio State University's hopes of winning the Big Ten by upending the Buckeyes on November 25, Northwestern grabbed the conference title. They were off to the big ball, the Rose Bowl, for the first time since 1947, against the 17th-ranked University of Southern California Trojans.

Alas, the clock struck midnight on New Year's Day, 1996, in Pasadena, California, where Northwestern's storybook season ended with a 41–32 loss.

1996

Michigan Finally Melts the Ice

College hockey typically has a tough time grabbing the headlines from football and basketball. Not so at the University of Michigan in the early 1990s. From 1993 to 1995, the Michigan Wolverines played to a 93–22–5 record. And when the team scored the winning goal in overtime to seal the 1996 NCAA championship against Colorado College on March 30, it generated even bigger news, because the Wolverines' hopes of skating to a national title had melted away in each of the last three NCAA hockey playoffs—all heartbreaking overtime losses.

The school had been a hockey powerhouse in the 1950s, winning five championships in six years from 1951 to 1956. But its last title had come 32 years ago. So when the 1996 Wolverines faced yet another overtime, in front of a crowd of 13,330 at Riverfront Coliseum in Cincinnati, they hoped recent history would not repeat itself.

At 3:35 into the overtime period, Brendan Morrison, a two-time All-America forward, rebounded a missed shot and fired the puck into the Colorado net. Final score: Michigan 3, Colorado 2. "We needed this for people to understand just how successful this program is," said Michigan coach Red Berenson. "Winning a national championship isn't easy."

Unbelieva-Bulls

Any doubts about Michael Jordan's worth to the Chicago Bulls were laid to rest during the 1995–1996 NBA season. With all due respect to Scottie Pippen, Toni Kukoc, Dennis Rodman, and the rest of the Bulls, they simply weren't the same team without Jordan. Not even close.

Jordan turned 33 in February, and age and the 17-month fling with baseball forced him to alter his game. His gravity-defying dunks went down less frequently, but refinement of a fade-away jump shot and career-best accuracy from three-point range (.427) more than made up for it. Jordan led the NBA in scoring (at 30.4 points per game) for a record eighth time in his career and won his fourth league MVP award.

As great as the Bulls were before Jordan left the first time (see page 37), this edition rewrote the record books. On February 27, with a 120–99 taming of the

Tiny Athlete, Big Heart *Injured Kerri Strug came to the victory stand in the arms of her coach, Bela Karolyi, after the U.S. women struck gymnastics gold (page 61).*

Minnesota Timberwolves, Chicago became the quickest team in North American professional sports history to reach 50 wins in a season. A come-from-behind victory over the Milwaukee Bucks on April 16 made the Bulls the first NBA team to achieve 70 wins; they finished the regular season at 72–10.

Chicago lost only one game in the first three rounds of the playoffs. Then, in the NBA Finals, the Bulls eliminated the Seattle SuperSonics in six games. The MVP of the best-of-seven championship series? Jordan, of course.

Jordan's greatness might seem almost robotic, yet he demonstrated very human emotion after the final buzzer sounded on June 16 at the United Center in Chicago. As the sold-out crowd cheered another NBA title, he grabbed the game ball and dashed to the Bulls' locker room. This was Jordan's first championship

1996

without his late father there to join in the celebration. Overcome with lingering grief, he lay on the floor in tears, clutching the basketball—on Father's Day.

The Olympics Comes to Atlanta

Boxing legend Muhammad Ali lit the torch at the Opening Ceremony to officially kick off the XXVIth Summer Olympic Games in Atlanta on July 19. Ali, a gold medalist at the 1960 Games in Rome and now a beloved figure worldwide, provided ideal illumination for the brilliant athletic achievements to come over the next two weeks. Although the Games were marred by a bomb at an Atlanta park on July 27 that left one person dead and 100 injured, and complaints of over-commercialization dogged local organizers, these Olympics were otherwise a success.

As with any Olympics, stories aplenty preceded the competition. Among the most compelling was speculation over whether American sprinter Michael Johnson (b.1967) would become the first male Olympian to win both the 200-meter and 400-meter races. He had already pulled off the double at the 1995 world championships, and track and field officials changed the Olympic schedule so he could attempt it again in Atlanta.

Johnson had "owned" the 400-meter event since 1989, winning 54 straight finals. But before the 1992 Olympics in Barcelona, Spain, he contracted a severe case of food poisoning that prevented him from competing. This time, he would not be denied. On July 29, he cruised to the gold medal, crossing the finish line with the largest margin of victory in the event in 10 years.

Two days later, Johnson made Olympic history in shimmering style. Wearing gold-colored running shoes, he stumbled slightly coming out of the starting blocks, but quickly recovered. Johnson already held the world record in the 200-meter race—set at 19.66 seconds in June—and when he kicked into hyperspeed about halfway through this race, he established an astonishing new mark of 19.32.

Gail Devers provided one of the most inspirational stories in Atlanta. A world-class sprinter and hurdler, she had overcome a serious thyroid disorder called Graves Disease, that sidelined her for two years (1989 to 1990) and nearly resulted in having both feet amputated. She not only returned to competition, but won the 100-meter sprint at the 1992 Olympics in a photo finish. At these Games, the same thing happened. Although Devers and Jamaica's Christine Ottey finished with identical times in the 100-meters, the judges declared Devers the gold medalist by the smallest of margins—an infinitesimal two centimeters.

At age 35, Carl Lewis, who had already won eight Olympic gold medals, took an unexpected ninth on July 29. He had won the long jump at the previous three Olympics, but he was not considered a contender this time. Nonetheless, on his third jump in the finals, he leaped into first place and then watched anxiously as the competition failed to beat him.

Americans captured a total of 44 gold medals in Atlanta, though none more heroically than in the team competition in women's gymnastics. The event combines the scores of each team's five athletes on the required apparatus (vault, uneven bars, balance beam, floor exercise). The U.S. team held a slight lead over the Russians as the United States competed on its last apparatus, the vault.

When the teammate before her faltered, 18-year-old Kerri Strug figured the gold depended on her performance. On her first attempt, she fell. Worse than that, she heard a sickening snap in her left ankle. That wasn't going to stop her, though. In excruciating pain and at the urging of her team, coach, and cheering spectators, Strug landed her next vault perfectly—then collapsed in agony. She had to be carried to the medal stand by her coach with a cast around her severely sprained ankle, as the gold medal was hung around her neck. Only later did Strug realize that the team would have won anyway, but that hardly diminished her gutsy feat.

Gymnastics wasn't the only sport in which a U.S. women's team achieved greatness. While the men's more-heralded Dream Team III breezed to the gold in basketball, the women hoopsters proved equally impressive. Undefeated in their yearlong pre-Olympic tour (52–0), they won all eight of their games in Atlanta, culminating with a convincing 111–87 victory over Brazil in the gold-medal match-up. The women's soccer team finished 4–0–1 in the first Olympic soccer tournament, including a riveting 2–1 win over China for the gold medal. The U.S. women also beat a strong Chinese team in the inaugural softball tournament final, 3–1. Dr. Dot Richardson, the team's 34-year-old shortstop and an orthopedic surgeon, made the difference with a two-run homer. Several controversial calls against the Chinese led to protests, but video reviews proved the umpires were correct.

American women were golden in the swimming pool, too. Leading the way was

MLS Kicks Off

Spurred by the popularity of the 1994 World Cup in America, soccer grew in stature in the decade, culminating with the launch of a new 10-team professional league, Major League Soccer, on April 6. Before a crowd of 31,683 at Spartan Stadium in San Jose, California, the hometown Clash outlasted Washington D.C. United, 1–0.

Fears that the league would fail, as several past attempts in the U.S. had, were soon put to rest when the Los Angeles Galaxy home opener against the New York/New Jersey MetroStars drew 69,255 to the Rose Bowl. For the 16-game season, the MLS attracted 2,786,673 fans, for a respectable average of 17,416 per contest—well over the projected 12,000 figure.

The MLS Cup championship game, on October 20 in front of 34,643 fans at rain-soaked, windswept Foxboro (Massachusetts) Stadium and a national TV audience, provided a thrilling climax to the inaugural season. The Galaxy and D.C. United played to a 2–2 tie at the end of regulation time. A little more than three minutes into the sudden-death overtime, D.C. United's Eddie Pope headed a corner kick for the winning goal. "Soccer fever is alive in the United States," said a jubilant D.C. United captain John Harkes during the post-game revelry, "and it's here to stay."

King of Swing

Pete Sampras dominated men's tennis during the 1990s. He burst onto the scene at the 1990 U.S. Open, one of the sport's four annual Grand Slam tournaments (the others are the Australian Open, the French Open, and Wimbledon). At 19 years, 28 days, he became the Open's youngest male winner, after dispensing with Ivan Lendl, John McEnroe, and Andre Agassi in the last three rounds. Sampras powered his way to 11 more Grand Slam titles during the decade, though perhaps none more memorable than back at the U.S. Open in 1996.

Born on August 12, 1971, in Washington, D.C., Sampras began playing tennis at age seven. He turned professional at 16 in 1988, won his first pro tournament in February 1990, and achieved the number-one ranking for the first of many times in April 1993. By the time he arrived back at the U.S. Open site at the National Tennis Center in Flushing, New York, for the 1996 event, Sampras had already won a half dozen more Grand Slam tournaments, including three straight Wimbledon titles (1993–1995). He also arrived with a heavy heart.

Tim Gullikson, Sampras' longtime coach, mentor, and close friend, had died of brain cancer in May. All year, a grieving Sampras had a hard time concentrating on his game. For the first time since 1992, he failed to win a Grand Slam. Then, on September 5 in the U.S. Open quarterfinal against 22-year-old Spaniard Alex Corretja, he played one of the most inspired matches in the history of the tournament. It went five sets and lasted four hours, nine minutes. Suffering from stomach cramps, Sampras vomited twice during the final set. Barely able to stand, much less serve and volley, he summoned up the energy to defeat Corretja. Three days later—on what would have been Gullikson's 45th birthday—Sampras beat Michael Chang for the title. "I've been thinking about him [Gullikson] all day and all during the match, about things he told me," Sampras said in the post-match press conference. "I still feel his spirit. He is still very much in my heart."

Sampras continued his masterful play over the remainder of the decade, winning four more Grand Slam titles. He also retained his number-one ranking, which he'd held since 1993, for a record six consecutive years, until 1998.

After losing to him in the Wimbledon final in 1999, Agassi was asked by the Associated Press whether Sampras was the greatest player ever. Agassi did not hesitate. "Yes," he said. "He's accomplished more than anybody else has, in my opinion. No question about it. His achievements speak for themselves."

---

the surprising 23-year-old Amy Van Dyken (b. 1973), whose childhood asthma was so bad, she used to collapse just walking up a flight of stairs. She took up swimming to increase her lung capacity, and by high school was a state champion. Her lungs worked just fine in Atlanta. She took individual golds in the 50-meter freestyle and 100-meter butterfly, and was a member of the U.S. teams that won the 4-by-100-meter freestyle and 4-by-100 medley relays.

Van Dyken thus became the first American woman to win four gold medals in one Olympic Games, either Summer or Winter. Teammate Jenny Thompson (b. 1973), who brought home two relay gold medals from the 1992 Olympic Games in Barcelona, Spain, picked up three more in the relays in Atlanta.

Tiger's Tale Grows

He was only two years old when he appeared on television's *Mike Douglas Show*, hitting golf balls with ageless comedian Bob Hope. The knee-high golf prodigy shot a 48 for nine holes at age three and was featured in *Golf Digest* magazine at age five. By 1996, Eldrick "Tiger" Woods (b.1975) had established himself as an emerging star. On August 25, he won an unprecedented third straight U.S. Amateur golf title in a spectacular fashion that would follow him into his record-setting professional career.

At Pumpkin Ridge Golf Club in North Plains, Oregon, Woods found himself five strokes down halfway through the 36-hole final match against University of Florida ace Steve Scott. The Tiger clawed his way back to a tie at the end of regulation play, then clinched his historic title on the second extra hole. The comeback capped a phenomenal amateur career in which he won three U.S. Junior Amateur championships. In two years at Stanford University (1995–1996), he won 10 collegiate events, including the NCAA golf title in 1996.

Two days after his smashing performance at Pumpkin Ridge, Woods turned pro by joining the Professional Golfers Association (PGA) tour at the Greater Milwaukee Open. He finished tied for 60th place, but more important, he made his much-anticipated professional debut (he had played in numerous pro tournaments since 1992, including the Masters and the U.S. Open, but with amateur status). The public had become fascinated not just with his amazing game,

but also his ethnicity. Woods' father is African-American, his mother is from Thailand. In a predominantly white sport, Woods was being compared to the late, great Jackie Robinson, who broke baseball's color barrier in 1947.

Woods, while confident in his abilities and aspirations, tried to downplay the race issue. "I'm not out just to be the best black player," he said. "I want to be the best golfer ever."

Before the year ended, Woods won two PGA events. On October 6, he held off Davis Love III in a sudden-death playoff to capture the Las Vegas Invitational. Two weeks later, at the Walt Disney World/Oldsmobile Classic in Orlando, he edged Payne Stewart for his second pro victory. Woods earned $940,420 in 11 tournaments worldwide and signed endorsement deals with Nike and Titleist worth $60 million. He was named the PGA Rookie of the Year and *Sports Illustrated's* Sportsman of the Year.

Sports Illustrated managing editor Bill Colson wrote an editorial explaining the choice of Woods over other remarkable athletes of 1996: "It seems clear, to us anyway, that one young man has recently surpassed all the others—perhaps in deeds but certainly in the long ripples those deeds produced. Tiger Woods, all of 20, all of four months as a pro under his belt after he won, in most dramatic fashion, a remarkable third straight U.S. Amateur title, is the only one among the candidates who changed the face of a sport, perhaps more rapidly than any other athlete ever has. In case you blinked and missed it, golf is no longer your father's sport."

On Top of the World *Third baseman Charlie Hayes and New York Yankees' fans celebrate the final out of the 1996 World Series. New York beat Atlanta in six games for its first title since 1978.*

Yankees Return from Series Slumber

The New York Yankees were already the 20th century's winningest baseball team, capturing 22 World Championships from 1923 to 1978, but the Bronx Bombers suffered through a slump from 1979 to 1995. That drought ended with the unpredictable 1996 World Series.

After winning back-to-back championships in 1977 and 1978, the Yankees returned to the Fall Classic following the strike-shortened 1981 season, but lost to the Los Angeles Dodgers in six games. Then came a string of futility from 1982 to 1994, during which New York failed to win the American League East (they were atop the division in 1994 before the strike ended the season) and changed managers a dozen times. They finally returned to the postseason in 1995, as the A.L.'s first wildcard entry, only to lose in the opening round to the Seattle Mariners.

Principal owner George Steinbrenner made yet another managerial switch before the 1996 season, naming Joe Torre (b.1940) as the 14th skipper of the ball club since Steinbrenner took the reigns in 1973. A 10-time All-Star player from 1960 to 1977, Torre had previously managed the New York Mets, Atlanta Braves, and St. Louis Cardinals, though with only modest success. But the Brooklyn native proved to be a perfect fit in the Bronx.

The Yankees finished the regular season in first place (92–70) and met the Texas Rangers in the best-of-five games divisional series in September. After losing game one at Yankee Stadium, New York won the next three to advance to the championship series against the Baltimore Orioles. With a little help from a hooky-playing 12-year-old—he leaned over the outfield wall to catch a fly ball that was incorrectly ruled a game-tying home run—the Yankees took game one and went on to wrap up the best-of-seven series in five games.

Meanwhile, over in the National League, the Atlanta Braves maintained their supremacy by wrapping up their fifth N.L. East title in the last six years (96–66). After sweeping the Los Angeles Dodgers in the divisional series, Atlanta staged a resilient comeback in the NLCS against the St. Louis Cardinals. Down three games to one, they roared to three straight victories, outscoring the Cardinals 32–1.

The Braves burst into Yankee Stadium on October 20 on a roll. They stunned their hosts 12–1 in game one, sparked by 19-year-old Andruw Jones, who hit home runs in his first two at-bats.

When Atlanta shut out the Yankees, 4–0, in game two—behind an 82-pitch, eight-inning gem from Greg Maddux—many wondered if New York was plainly outmatched. Not quite, as the Yankees won three straight games in Atlanta. The Series took a dramatic turn in game four when New York battled back from a 6–0 deficit; the decisive moment was a three-run homer by Jim Leyritz in the eighth inning to tie the score. The Yanks prevailed, 8–6, in 10 innings.

Game six finally produced a win for the home team, with the Yankees taking it—and their first Series in 18 years. Torre, perhaps sensing a measure of job security, said after the deciding contest, "Second place is not an option with George Steinbrenner, which is fine by me."

Other Milestones of 1996

✔ The University of Nebraska, on the heels of a 62–24 pasting of number two University of Florida in the Fiesta Bowl on January 2, became the first college football team in 16 years to win back-to-back national championships.

✔ Don Shula, head coach of the Miami Dolphins since 1970, resigned on January 5. His legacy included an NFL-record 347 wins, two Super Bowl titles (VII and VIII), and the only perfect record (17–0 in 1972) in NFL history.

✔ The Dallas Cowboys beat the Pittsburgh Steelers, 27–17, in Super Bowl XXX on January 28 at Sun Devil Stadium in Tempe, Arizona.

✔ On February 8, the NFL approved the Cleveland Browns' move to Baltimore, but ruled that the team's

Nebraska quarterback Frankie London

colors and name must remain in Cleveland for use by a future franchise.

✔ Kentucky topped Syracuse, 76–67, to win the NCAA men's basketball championship on April 1. It marked the Wildcats' sixth national title.

✔ In the final round of the Masters golf tournament on April 14, Greg Norman blew a six-shot lead and was overtaken by eventual winner Nick Faldo.

✔ Seattle Mariners shortstop Alex Rodriguez, the top pick in the 1993 draft, hit .358 with 36 home runs and 123 runs batted in, fulfilling the promise many had seen in his play.

✔ Boxer Evander Holyfield scored a surprising 11th-round technical knockout of Mike Tyson to gain the heavyweight title on November 9.

1997

The Pack Is Back

It's not too hard to figure out why Green Bay, Wisconsin, is affectionately known as Titletown. The hometown Packers, after all, won 11 NFL titles from 1929 to 1967, plus the first two Super Bowls following the 1966 and 1967 seasons. Alas, after that glorious high point under legendary coach Vince Lombardi (1913–1970), the town went without any titles for the next 28 years. So when the Packers outscored the New England Patriots, 35–21, to win Super Bowl XXXI on January 26 at the Superdome in New Orleans, Titletown was its old self again.

Balance was the hallmark of this 13–3 Packers team, the first since the 1972 Miami Dolphins to lead the league in most points scored (456) and fewest points allowed (210). Quarterback Brett Favre (b.1969) won his second straight NFL MVP award after throwing an NFC-record 39 touchdowns to several receivers. Veteran defensive end Reggie White was the bedrock of the defense.

The 11–5 Patriots marched into the Superdome with a high-flying passing game directed by quarterback Drew Bledsoe (b.1972). Curtis Martin rushed for 1,152 yards and 14 touchdowns during the season. Still, New England was the underdog when Super Bowl XXXI kicked off. After quickly falling behind 10–0, the Patriots scored 14 points to take the lead after one quarter.

Less than a minute into the second quarter, Favre tossed a Super Bowl-record, 81-yard touchdown bomb to Antonio Freeman. The Packers scored another 10 points before halftime. Undaunted, the Patriots crept to within six points on Martin's 18-yard touchdown run late in the third quarter, but then Green Bay's Desmond Howard snapped their spirit with a 99-yard return of the ensuing kickoff. A two-point conversion capped off the scoring—and the triumphant back-to-Titletown season for the Packers.

The Fresh Prince of NASCAR

He didn't have the Southern pedigree of Richard Petty, the recently retired King of stock car racing (see page 32). But clean-cut Midwesterner Jeff Gordon (b.1971), like Petty, became a royal pain in the neck to his fellow NASCAR competitors. In 1997, Gordon, the kid from

Sunday Drive *Tiger Woods left no doubt he was golf's next superstar with a whopping 12-stroke victory at the prestigious Masters tournament (page 69).*

Pittsboro, Indiana, just kept winning races, especially the big ones.

Gordon got his engine running right at the start of the Winston Cup season, winning the Daytona 500 on February 14. He promised team owner Rick Hendrick, who was back home in North Carolina fighting leukemia, that he'd win the race. Not only did Gordon, at age 25, become the youngest driver to win NASCAR's

Boy Wonder *Twenty-five-year-old Jeff Gordon won his first Daytona 500 in 1997 and went on dominate the NASCAR circuit en route to winning driver-of-the-year honors.*

Gordon went on to post one of the most remarkable seasons in NASCAR history. He took nine more of the 31 races on the Winston Cup circuit, winning $4,201,227 along the way. Plus, he finished first in two of the other four major races: the Coca-Cola 600 and the Southern 500 (the fourth is the Winston 500). That earned him the Winston Million—a cool $1 million bonus—which had only been won once before, by "Dollar" Bill Elliott in 1985. With the princely sum of his season, Gordon was easily crowned Winston Cup driver of the year.

In the 'Zona

This year's NCAA men's basketball tournament said a lot about the changing face of college hoops. More and more players were leaving school early to enter the NBA draft, making "senior leadership" (where the older players take the lead on the court) less of a factor. And some high school superstars, such as Kevin Garnett (b.1976) and Kobe Bryant (b.1978), bypassed college altogether, going straight to the pros. That meant younger, less experienced players had to carry more of the load in the college game.

Critics charged that this trend ultimately brought down the overall level of college competition. Defenders countered that parity was now the name of the game, with more schools having better chances to win.

So when the University of Arizona Wildcats—a number four seed in the tournament and number 15 in the country—and only the fifth-best team in its

most prestigious event, but he led a one-two-three sweep of Hendrick-team cars (Terry Labonte and Rickey Craven finished second and third, respectively).

Less fortunate was Dale Earnhardt (1952–2001), who was still looking for his first Daytona win in 19 tries. Gordon passed Earnhardt for second place with 10 laps to go, and the move set in motion a huge crash that left Earnhardt's car a mangled mess. Instead of taking himself out of the race, though, Earnhardt climbed back inside the wreck, restarted the car, and finished 31st.

Pacific-10 Conference—beat the number-one-seeded Wildcats from the University of Kentucky in the final game, it really wasn't considered much of an upset. Indeed, Arizona accepted the trophy as a very deserving champion. Its six tournament wins included victories over two other top seeds and perennial powerhouses, the University of Kansas and North Carolina University. It also marked the first time in tournament history that one team knocked off three number-one seeds on the road to the title.

The NCAA tournament featured the usual first-round upsets: number 15 seed Coppin State University surprised second-seeded University of South Carolina; number 14 seed University of Tennessee at Chattanooga upset number three University of Georgia; number 12 seed College of Charleston beat number five University of Maryland. Even so, three of the number-one seeds advanced to the Final Four at the RCA Dome in Indianapolis, March 29 and 31.

In the semifinals, defending national champion Kentucky beat the University of Minnesota for the right to meet Arizona (which defeated North Carolina) two nights later. Although Kentucky coach Rick Pitino's Wildcats were favored over the Arizona, coached by Lute Olson, statistically the teams were pretty evenly matched. Kentucky's edge was experience from last year's Final Four, even though six players from that team were gone. Olson's best player was junior guard Miles Simon, but he depended on freshman point guard Mike Bibby to run the team.

Arizona led by one point at halftime, 33–32. With 61 seconds left in the game,

Arizona was up 72–68, seemingly on their way to the school's first national basketball championship. But Kentucky's Ron Mercer and Anthony Epps each hit three-pointers; Arizona could only score two more points for the tie, and the game went into overtime. Kentucky lost its earlier momentum in the five-minute extra period and was forced to foul. Arizona kept its cool, sank enough free throws, and prevailed, 84–79.

Both teams were composed mostly of freshman and sophomores whose relatively raw talent brought them this far. Yet this tournament, wrote Paul Attner in *The Sporting News*, "provided a wonderful road map to show us where the sport is headed after too many years of losing too many elite underclassmen to the NBA."

Tiger Tames Augusta

The golf world had been waiting for this moment, for Tiger Woods to take on the man-eating course at Augusta National Golf Club in Augusta, Georgia. But with his record-setting 12-stroke victory in the annual Masters Tournament, April 10 to 13, it could be an eternity before we see another such masterful performance. The 21-year-old golf genius made Augusta seem like a miniature golf course.

Woods' incredible golfing performance came on what is considered to be among the most challenging courses in the sport. Augusta's long, narrow fairways, treacherous bunkers, and rolling greens have tested and taunted the best players in the game ever since legendary

We've Come A Long Way

The other remarkable aspect of Tiger Woods' phenomenal win at Augusta had to do with his ethnicity (half African-American, half Thai) and its sociological implications. An excerpt from an article written the following day by *Philadelphia Inquirer* sports columnist Bill Lyon poignantly summarized the significance of the occasion:

> Tiger Woods won a tournament of great prestige in one of the most exclusive and restrictive enclaves in the world, a place that, until recent years, he could have gained admission to only by way of the servant's entrance.
>
> The green-coated autocrats of Augusta National would have permitted him to clean their ashtrays and shine their shoes and serve them assorted beverages. But the only way he would have set a shoe onto those lush and fragrant fairways was as a caddy.
>
> Last night, in the gentle Georgia gloaming, those very same men stood to applaud as Tiger Woods slipped into a coat of the very same hue as theirs. They shook the hand of a 21-year-old prodigy, and their grip was sincere. The optimist in you would like to think that at that moment, we edged another inch up the progress chart.
>
> It will be recorded that, two days before the 50th anniversary of Jackie Robinson first playing in a Major League Baseball game, Woods became the first African American to win a Masters or, indeed, any major golf tournament.
>
> But this is too narrow, too constricting. Because through Tiger Woods courses the blood of five nationalities—not only African-American, but Chinese, Cherokee, Thai, and Dutch. Tiger Woods is a melting pot with a wedge.
>
> Better, then, that we celebrate him, and this, for what they are—a triumph for all humankind.

golfer Bobby Jones created the course and the tournament in 1934.

Woods got off to a shaky start in the four-day tournament. He shot 40 on the first nine holes of the 18-hole course, but then settled into a groove. That's an understatement. Over the next three days and 63 holes, he shot 22 under par, finishing 18 under to break the great Jack Nicklaus' (b. 1940) and Ray Floyd's Masters record. His 12-stroke win was the largest margin of victory in a major tournament since Tom Morris won the 1862 British Open by 13 strokes. (Besides the Masters and the British Open, the two other majors are the U.S. Open and the PGA Championship.)

"He's out there playing another game on a golf course he is going to own for a long time," said Nicklaus, who won the Masters at age 23 and whose six titles are more than anyone else's—so far.

A Basketball League of Their Own

The eight-team Women's National Basketball Association (WNBA), an affiliate of the NBA, tipped off its inaugural season on June 21 as the New York Liberty beat the Los Angeles Sparks, 67–57. A crowd of 14,284 at the Great Western Forum, in Inglewood, California, witnessed Sparks guard Penny Toler score the first basket in WNBA history.

A hybrid of the pro and college games, the WNBA features a 30-second shot clock, a 19-foot, nine-inch three-point line, two 20-minute halves, 11-player rosters, and a signature orange-and-oatmeal, collegiate-size basketball

(28.5 inches in circumference, one inch smaller than the NBA's regulation ball).

The teams, with recent college stars such as Lisa Leslie, Rebecca Lobo, Sheryl Swoopes, and Cynthia Cooper, played 28 games in 1997. On August 30, the Houston Comets, led by league MVP Cooper's 25 points, defeated the Liberty, 65–51, to capture the first WNBA title.

The Fall of Tyson, Part II

By the time he stepped into the boxing ring against Evander Holyfield on June 28, Mike Tyson had experienced a wild range of highs and lows, in and out of boxing. Right from the start of his professional career in 1985, Tyson's power-punching, street-fighting style intimidated opponents. He won 14 fights that year, 11 by first-round knockouts. A year later, "Iron Mike" won the World Boxing Council (WBC) heavyweight title, becoming the youngest heavyweight fighter, at age 20, to win a world title. By the end of 1987 he held the WBC, World Boxing Association (WBA), and International Boxing Federation (IBF) titles, making him the undisputed heavyweight champion.

In the meantime, his personal life took a beating. A brief and turbulent marriage to actress Robin Givens ended in divorce. In 1992, two years after his shocking loss to relative unknown Buster Douglas, he was convicted of raping an 18-year-old woman and served three years in prison. Tyson regained his WBC and WBA titles in 1996, but then lost the WBA title in November to Holyfield. Now came the rematch, which turned into one of sports' more bizarre spectacles.

Reality Bites *Champion Evander Holyfield grimaces while bitten by challenger Mike Tyson in their heavyweight title fight. Tyson was fined and suspended, but soon was back in the boxing ring.*

The arena at the MGM Grand Garden in Las Vegas was packed for the greatly anticipated fight. Holyfield won the first two rounds on all three judges' scorecards. As Tyson prepared to come out for the third round, Holyfield pointed out that he'd forgotten his mouthpiece. Once the fight resumed, Tyson spit out the mouthpiece, grabbed Holyfield, and bit his right ear. The action had to be halted for four minutes while the ringside doctor tended to Holyfield's bleeding ear. But after the fight started up again, Tyson did the same thing, except this time he bit Holyfield's left ear.

Referee Mills Lane immediately stopped the fight and disqualified Tyson. While Holyfield went to the hospital for treatment, Tyson defended his actions, charging that Holyfield had illegally head-butted him in the first and second

More Unruly Behavior

Mike Tyson wasn't the only sports personality who couldn't control himself this year:

- In game five of the NBA Eastern Conference semifinals on May 14 in Miami, players from the New York Knicks and Miami Heat got into a bench-clearing brawl. The league suspended the Heat's P. J. Brown and the Knicks' Patrick Ewing, Charlie Ward, and Allan Houston for game six; Brown and the Knicks' Larry Johnson and John Starks were suspended for game seven. The Knicks, up a commanding three games to one coming into game five, lost that game and the series.

- On September 25, veteran sportscaster Marv Albert pleaded guilty to misdemeanor assault and battery charges. It was revealed during the trial in Virginia that Albert had bitten his female accuser during sex. Hours after the verdict, he was fired from his announcer's job at NBC Sports and resigned as an announcer for the Madison Square Garden Network.

- Latrell Sprewell (b.1970), a guard for basketball's Golden State Warriors, punched and choked his head coach, P.J. Carlesimo, during practice on December 1. Sprewell claimed that he was provoked by ongoing verbal abuse from Carlesimo. In one of the most costly punishments in sports history, the NBA suspended Sprewell for one year and the Warriors terminated the remaining three years of his four-year, $32 million contract.

rounds. State boxing officials suspended Tyson and withheld his $30 million fee for the fight, pending an inquiry.

On July 9, the Nevada Athletic Commission revoked Tyson's boxing license for one year and fined him $3 million—which meant he ended up making $27 million. Tyson's Nevada boxing license was restored October 19, 1998, and he was back in the ring by January of the following year.

The One-Year Wonders

By winning the 1997 World Series, team owner H. Wayne Huizenga and his Florida Marlins proved that baseball in the 1990s had unmistakably become a game in which money talks. Following the 1995 season, which the Marlins finished with a record of 67–76, Huizenga devised a two-year upgrade plan. The owner of Blockbuster Video stores opened up his ample wallet to sign top pitchers Kevin Brown and Al Leiter in 1996 and Alex Fernandez in 1997. He bulked up the offense by adding Moises Alou, Darren Daulton, and Bobby Bonilla to the 1997 roster. The critical move, though, was hiring manager Jim Leyland, a proven winner who had navigated the Pittsburgh Pirates to three consecutive National League East titles from 1990 to 1992. Coupled with other complimentary acquisitions and its budding homegrown talent, Florida was poised to make a pennant run this year.

Behind strong pitching, Florida won a team-best 92 games during the regular season. That was second in the N.L. East to the 101–61 Atlanta Braves, but enough to qualify as the N.L. wildcard entry in the playoffs. The Marlins swept the San Francisco Giants in three games in the division series, then surprised the mighty Braves by taking the N.L. Championship Series (NLCS), four games to two in September.

The Cleveland Indians won the American League pennant with a power-packed lineup. Sluggers Jim Thome, Matt Williams, David Justice, Manny Ramirez, and Sandy Alomar Jr. led an offense that produced enough runs to overpower a mediocre pitching staff. Cleveland won the A.L. Central with an 86–75 record, knocked off the New York Yankees in the divisional series, and beat the Baltimore Orioles in six games in the ALCS.

The World Series came down to a thrilling seventh game on October 26 in Miami. In the bottom of the 11th inning, with the score tied 2–2, Florida shortstop Edgar Renteria hit a two-out, bases-loaded single off Charles Nagy to score Greg Counsell. Thus the Marlins, in just their fifth season, became the quickest expansion team to win the World Series.

Baseball-wise, Huizenga's investments paid major dividends. Financially, however, the owner complained that he'd lost $30 million and wanted to sell the team. Ironically, to make the sale more attractive—that is, to lower the price of the team—he began unloading players within weeks after the Series. On Opening Day of 1998, an almost entirely new team took the field, leaving dismayed fans with only fleeting memories of glory. The Marlins went on the finish with the worst record in baseball, at 54–108. The following January, the team was sold.

Other Milestones of 1997

✔ Quarterback Danny Wuerffel, the 1996 Heisman Trophy winner, led the University of Florida to its first Division I college football national title following the school's 52–20 trouncing of rival Florida State University in the Sugar Bowl on January 2.

✔ The University of Tennessee's Lady Vols, paced by Chamique Holdsclaw's 24 points, topped Old Dominion University, 68–59, on March 30 to repeat as college basketball national champions.

✔ On June 13, the Chicago Bulls won their fifth NBA title of the 1990s. They beat the Utah Jazz, 90–86, in Chicago to take the series, 4–2. Michael Jordan was the MVP, averaging 32.3 points per game.

✔ After 36 seasons, Dean Smith retired as head basketball coach at the

Charles Woodson

University of North Carolina on October 9. In his career, he won a record 879 games, two NCAA titles, and 17 Atlantic Coast Conference titles.

✔ After 56 years as the head coach at Grambling State University in north-central Louisiana, the legendary Eddie Robinson retired November 29. His last game was a loss (30-7 to rival Southern University in the Bayou Classic), but the 78-year-old finished his career as college football's all-time winningest coach with a record of 408-165-15. Robinson fashioned three perfect seasons at the small, historically African-American college and won eight black national championships.

✔ On December 13, University of Michigan cornerback Charles Woodson became the first primarily defensive player to win the Heisman Trophy, awarded to college football's best player

1998

Broncos Kick It Up

After four unsuccessful tries—three with John Elway (b.1960) at quarterback—the Denver Broncos finally won a Super Bowl. They upset the favored Green Bay Packers, 31–24, in Super Bowl XXXII, on January 25 at Qualcomm Stadium in San Diego. Elway, 37 years old, at long last had a Vince Lombardi trophy and a championship ring—the missing pieces to go along with reams of spectacular statistics amassed over his 16 NFL seasons. Denver also brought relief for long-suffering American Football Conference (AFC) teams, which had dropped 13 straight Super Bowls to National Football Conference (NFC) teams.

The Broncos qualified for the playoffs as a wildcard contender with a 12–4 record in the AFC Western Division. They mauled the Jacksonville Jaguars in the first round, 42–17. Then they ground out a pair of close, impressive road wins, against the Kansas City Chiefs (14–10) and the Pittsburgh Steelers (24–21), for the right to meet Green Bay in San Diego. The reigning champion Packers, behind a third consecutive NFL MVP season by quarterback Brett Favre, confidently strutted into the stadium with a 13–3 regular-season record and impressive playoff wins over the Tampa Bay Buccaneers (21–7) and the San Francisco 49ers (23–10).

In each of Elway's Super Bowl defeats (XXI, XXII, XXIV), the future Hall of Fame quarterback did all he could to carry the team on his golden arm and scrambling legs, only to watch the Broncos' running game stumble.

This time, Elway only needed to be efficient (he passed for 123 yards and ran for a touchdown), thanks to running back Terrell Davis and an offensive line that could make a hole in anything. The AFC's top rusher that season (1,750 yards), Davis tortured the Packers' defense, gaining 157 yards on 30 carries and scoring a Super Bowl-record three rushing touchdowns—despite being sidelined most of the second quarter with a migraine headache. His one-yard dive into the end zone with a 1:45 left in the game broke a 24–24 tie. For his valiant effort, Davis was voted the game's MVP.

Even so, it was Elway who garnered much of the post-game attention. "I'm happy for him," said Favre. "He's had a great career and he's finally got the greatest thing that the NFL has to offer."

Rocky Mountain High *Quarterback John Elway was on top of the world after leading Denver to a Super Bowl win.*

New Games in the Winter Olympics

From February 7 to 22, the modest mountain city of Nagano, Japan, a little more than an hour northwest of Tokyo, hosted 2,302 athletes from 72 countries as they participated in 68 events in the Winter Olympic Games. Among them were,

for the first time as official medal sports, snowboarding, curling, and women's ice hockey. The United States won 13 medals at Nagano: six gold, three silver, and four bronze.

The super-fast Super G (giant slalom) course at the Hakuba downhill skiing venue provided one of the most golden moments of the Games for the United

Upside Down *The 1998 Winter Olympics in Nagano, Japan, were host to a number of new medal sports. Among them: the extreme sport of snowboarding, a staple of the X Games.*

States. That's where Picabo Street turned previous tragedies into triumph. Only 14 months earlier, Street had crashed while training in Vail, Colorado, damaging ligaments, cartilage, and bone in her left knee. She ·recovered from reconstructive surgery in remarkable time, and began training for Nagano just before Thanksgiving 1997. Then, 11 days before the Olympics began, Street fell on a slope in Sweden and was knocked unconscious.

Her first of two events in Japan was the downhill, in which she took the silver

medal at the 1994 Games in Lillehammer, Norway. When she was on the medal stand listening to the German national anthem being played for gold medalist Katja Seizinger, she thought to herself, "Next time I'm back up here, I'm going to be listening to my national anthem played for me." But it was not to be in the downhill, as Street finished sixth. Still, she kept her hopes high for the upcoming Super G.

Wearing a skintight, blazing yellow suit and racing on longer downhill skis, Street had a slight misstep about halfway through her final run, but recovered nicely. Her time of 1:18.02 put her in first place, though her toughest competitors had yet to ski. Austria's Michaela Dorfmeister crossed the finish line at 1:18.03—giving Street the gold by a scant one one-hundredth of a second, the slimmest margin of victory possible. A short while later, she was beaming atop the medal stand to the strains of "The Star Spangled Banner."

Meanwhile, in the figure skating hall, 15-year-old Tara Lipinski skated her short program to a song from the movie *Anastasia*. She did well, but her favored rival, fellow American Michelle Kwan (b.1980), skated slightly better and was in first place going into the decisive long program two nights later. Kwan went first among the six finalists and turned in what appeared to be a winning performance. Lipinski, who came to Nagano determined to soak up the total experience and simply let it all hang out in competition, skated a nearly flawless program. Her squeals of joy, as she saw her scores come up indicating she'd captured the gold medal, echoed throughout the arena.

A lot of women took to the ice for the first Olympic women's hockey tournament, which came down to a face-off between the United States and Canada. Throughout the 1990s the Canadians had dominated the sport, especially against the Americans, beating them in four world championships. Canada was fully expected to maintain its mastery in Nagano.

The two teams met earlier in the Olympic tournament, with the Americans prevailing, 7–4, in an ugly contest marred by too many penalties and too much trash talk. The rematch in the final was more civil. The United States won, 3–1, with clean, hard skating, solid goaltending, and timely goals. Sarah Tueting in the net registered 21 saves, and the goals were scored by Gretchen Ulion, Shelley Looney, and Danielle Goyette.

Back on the ski slopes, the United States took three of the four gold medals in freestyle skiing. Eric Bergoust and Nikki Stone won the men's and women's aerials, respectively. Bergoust, with his gravity-defying aerobatics, set a world record with a pair of nearly perfect quadruple twisting triple flips. Stone nailed both her back somersaults to top the 12-woman field. Jonny Moseley, a free-spirited Californian, won the freestyle moguls event on the strength of his trademark helicopter jump — a 360-degree spin in the air while grabbing one of his crossed skis, followed by a pinpoint landing.

Bowling for Dollars

SBig-time college sports programs, primarily football and basketball, are big-time not just because they produce star athletes and entertaining games. They also generate millions of dollars in annual revenue for participating schools. Most of the money spills over from huge, multi-year broadcast-rights deals between television networks and the various conferences to which the schools belong. For instance, CBS had a $1.725 billion, seven-year deal that ran until 2002 to televise the NCAA men's basketball tournament (in November 1999, CBS negotiated a new $6-billion, 11-year contract with the NCAA). Every school that participates in the tournament enjoys a piece of the pie.

College football's ever-growing slate of post-season bowl games are tremendous money makers, too. The bowl format, though, has undergone tinkering in recent years in an attempt to decide a true national champion. Previously, the "champion" was declared by rival polls taken among sportswriters and coaches. Occasionally, those polls disagreed about the national champion, leading to endless debates. However, regular proposals for a playoff system, as in college hoops, have been squashed, in large part because of the fear of losing large payouts offered by traditional postseason bowl games.

In 1998, in the latest scheme to pair the No. 1 and No. 2 teams in the land in a single "championship" game, officials from the Orange, Sugar, Rose, and Fiesta bowls joined with the Atlantic Coast, Big East, Big 12, Big Ten, Pacific-10, and Southeastern conferences and the University of Notre Dame to form the Bowl Championship Series (BCS). A complex system, using national polls, computer tabulations, and strength of schedules, ranks teams and ultimately determines the bowl

1998

match-ups. The national championship game rotates each year among the four BCS bowls.

The pressure to play in the BCS is overwhelming and goes beyond the bounds of athletic competition. ABC has a deal worth more than $930 million to broadcast the games through January 2006. Each team that makes it to the BCS will earn about $13 million, a figure that will rise to nearly $17 million by the end of the agreement. Lesser bowls pay out around $1 million per team.

All this money floating around perpetuated attacks on college sports and the influence on school officials and coaches to produce winning programs. Academic integrity suffers in the quest for athletic power, prestige, and money, numerous critics charged.

The issue became even more contentious in 2003, when the Atlantic Coast Conference wooed away the University of Miami and Virginia Tech University from the Big East Conference. Miami, the reigning national football champs, was certain to add to the ACC's coffers while reducing the Big East's. In other words, some schools would benefit at the expense of others. The maneuver fostered acrimony between schools in the two conferences, fears that similar defections would follow, and further negativism surrounding the state of big-time college sports. (For more, see page 103.)

Big E for Endurance

NASCAR could not have planned a more perfect beginning for its 50th anniversary season, as the sport's most popular driver won its most prestigious event—finally. After 19 hope-filled tries and 19 frustrating failures, Dale Earnhardt succeeded in taking the checkered flag at the Daytona 500. "The Intimidator," as the hard-driving, highly competitive Earnhardt was known, already had seven Winston Cup driving championships, 70 career Cup wins, and 575 Cup starts under his seatbelt, including 30 on the hallowed, high-banked oval track at Daytona, Florida.

Earnhardt was 46 years old when he climbed into his famous black No. 3 Chevy on February 15, 1998. Since becoming NASCAR's Winston Cup Rookie of the Year in 1979, he had won just about every other race, but was on the brink of be-

Long Time Coming *Legendary Dale Earnhardt (in the number-3 car) won the biggest race on the NASCAR circuit, the Daytona 500, for the first time on his 20th try.*

The Man in Black

There was little doubt, when he was growing up in tiny Kannapolis, North Carolina, that Dale Earnhardt would some day race cars for a living. His father, Ralph Earnhardt, was one of stock car racing's pioneers during the 1950s, and young Dale soaked up the rough-and-tumble lifestyle. "I wanted to race—that's all I ever wanted to do," he once said. "I didn't care about work or school or anything. All I wanted to do was to work on race cars and then drive race cars. It was always my dream, and I was just fortunate enough to be able to live out that dream."

True to his word, Earnhardt quit school when he was 16 and made his Winston Cup debut in 1975, finishing 22nd in the World 600 at the Charlotte Motor Speedway in North Carolina. He joined NASCAR's "major league" circuit full-time in 1979. Earnhardt took his first Winston Cup win that season at Bristol Motor Speedway in Bristol, Tennessee, and was named Rookie of the Year. A year later, he became the first Winston Cup driver to win Rookie of the Year and Driver of the Year in successive seasons.

Along with six more championships, he claimed victory in nearly every major event on the circuit, including a career-best 11 wins in 1987. In 2000, when some wondered if he'd passed his prime, Earnhardt posted two wins, 13 top five finishes, and 24 top 10s, and came in second behind Jeff Gordon in the final points standings.

On February 18, 2001, Earnhardt started his 23rd Daytona 500 from the seventh position and was racing for third during the last lap. He had himself in position so that his teammate, Michael Waltrip, and his son, Dale Earnhardt Jr., would finish first and second, respectively. Suddenly, Dale Sr.'s No. 3 Chevy was bumped by another car, causing Earnhardt to crash head-on into the wall. He was killed instantly.

Wrote *AutoWeek* managing editor Roger Hart in tribute, "As we found out February 18 at the Daytona International Speedway, even being the best of the best—and make no mistake about it, Dale Earnhardt was the best stock car driver ever—is not always enough. Like many other race fans across the country, I will miss Dale Earnhardt. NASCAR racing will not be the same. He helped make stock car racing what it is today, and if there's any solace in his passing, it's that he loved every minute of it."

coming one of those sports legends who never wins The Big One.

Earnhardt had been oh-so-close to winning Daytona before. Four times he'd lost the lead with 10 laps to go. He'd come up short twice on the last lap. This year, he had a pack of pesky pursuers on his tail as the 200-lap race neared its exciting conclusion. He held them all off, though, and a long-awaited celebration erupted. To conclude his most memorable victory lap, Earnhardt cruised down pit road (the stretch alongside a racetrack where pit crews are stationed), as drivers and crew members from virtually every team lined up to shake his hand. Then he went into the infield and did a couple of celebratory donuts (spinning his car in circles).

"I wish every race driver that ever runs Daytona could feel what we felt yesterday in Victory Lane," Earnhardt told reporters the following day. "That's one of the greatest feelings in your life, to work that many years and come so close and be so dominant and finally win that race. It's an accomplishment I won't forget."

1998

Beísbol in America

The Hispanic presence in Major League Baseball had been quietly growing since the 1970s. A small handful of players had appeared before that, most notably Hall of Famer Roberto Clemente (1934–1972) from Puerto Rico. In the 1990s, however, their numbers multiplied. In 1998, for instance, for the first time, the MVPs of both leagues were born in Latin American countries: for the National League, Sammy Sosa from the Dominican Republic; for the American League, Puerto Rico native Juan Gonzalez.

From 1990 to 2001, according to Northeastern University's Center for the Study of Sport in Society director, Peter Roby, the number of Hispanic major leaguers swelled to 26 percent from 13 percent; most were born outside the U.S. In the same period, the number of African Americans on Major League Baseball rosters declined to 13 percent from 17 percent and the percentage of white players shrank to 59 from 70. This reflected similar trends in the general U.S. population.

Dating back to the 1860s, baseball has a long and rich tradition in Cuba, the Dominican Republic, Puerto Rico, and other Latin American nations. Some Major League baseball teams used to have spring training camps and play exhibition games there. But not until about the same time Jackie Robinson broke the game's color barrier in 1947, did foreign-born Hispanics catch scouts' eyes. Over the coming decades, some would shine as among baseball's best, including Hall of Famers Juan Marichal (Dominican Republic), Rod Carew (Panama), Orlando Cepeda (Puerto Rico), Tony Perez (Cuba), and Luis Tiant (Cuba).

Hispanics continued to thrive, if not in numbers, then in stature, until the 1990s. That's when economics led to a tremendous influx of talented Latin players who could be signed for far less money than what U.S. high school and college prospects commanded. By the end of the decade, virtually every major league franchise had opened baseball academies in the Dominican Republic, by far the region's greatest pool of talent. Besides Sosa, the island nation had by then produced such marquee names as Pedro Martinez, Manny Ramirez, Miguel Tejada, Raul Mondesi, and Jose Rijo.

Hispanics on the 1998 All-Star teams included Sosa, Gonzalez, Alex Rodriguez, Ivan Rodriguez, brothers Roberto and Sandy Alomar, Moises Alou, Andres Galarraga, Javy Lopez, and Edgar Renteria. Second baseman Roberto Alomar—on the strength of his home run, walk, stolen base, and superb defensive play—won the MVP Award for the '98 All-Star game, which the A.L. won, 13–8.

Lady Vols, Take Three

Women's sports flourished during the 1990s. From Little League to the Olympics, female athletes participated in ever-increasing numbers at higher and higher levels of competition. The highest profile sport for women was college basketball, which ran a fast break through the decade. And by winning their third straight NCAA national championship on March 29 at Kemper Arena in Kansas City, Missouri, the University of Tennessee's Lady Vols exemplified just how far the sport had advanced.

Coached by the celebrated Pat Summitt, in her 24th year at Tennessee, the Lady Vols steamrolled through the regular season undefeated, 33–0. They utterly dominated opponents, outscoring teams by an average margin of 30.1 points per game.

Chamique Holdsclaw, the junior forward and national player of the year, solidified her reputation as perhaps the best female college player ever. "Her Airness" — as she had become known, borrowing a nickname from Michael Jordan — not only averaged 23.5 points per game (including six NCAA tournament appearances), but demonstrated tremendous leadership to a pair of talented, but raw freshmen, Tamika Catchings and Semeka Randall.

The tournament's field of 64 teams showcased the burgeoning talent found at schools nationwide, but Tennessee was clearly at the head of the class. Its only speedbump along the road to Kansas City came in the Mideast Regional final versus the University of North Carolina, in which the Vols valiantly overcame a 12-point second-half deficit to prevail, 76–70. They played a near-perfect championship game, easily dispensing with Louisiana Tech University, 93–75. Holdsclaw — with 25 points, 10 rebounds, and six assists in the finale — was voted the Final Four's Most Outstanding Player.

Tennessee thus became the first women's team to claim three straight titles, and it was their sixth in 12 years.

"The best team doesn't always win," said Summitt in the post-game press conference, "but tonight, I thought the best team won a championship that they deserved."

Chasing 61

After the players' strike wiped out the last quarter of the 1994 Major League Baseball season and all of the post-season, including the World Series, observers wondered if baseball would ever win back the hearts of jilted fans. In

The Repeat Threepeat

The Lady Vols weren't the only basketball team to pull off a rare back-to-back-to-back championship in 1998. In the NBA, the Chicago Bulls clinched their third straight title on June 14, eliminating the Utah Jazz in six games. It was the Bulls' second three-peat of the 1990s, Chicago having also enjoyed a triumphant trio from 1991 to 1993. The two-year hiatus, not surprisingly, came during the absence of Michael Jordan.

No surprise, either, that Jordan once again set the pace, for the Bulls and the league. He added to his super-sized trophy case a fifth NBA MVP award and his 10th scoring title, averaging 28.7 points per game (35.0 in the finals). It was his final shot of the season, however, that was heard around the basketball world. In game six of the finals, at the Delta Center in Salt Lake City, the Jazz were up by one point in the last few seconds. Jordan got his hands on the ball, shook off defender Byron Russell, and drilled the title-winning shot that not only sealed Utah's coffin, but Jordan's career. The following January 13, he retired . . . again . . . maybe.

Actually, that shot and that game marked the demise of the Bulls' dynastic decade. Among those departing along with Jordan were head coach Phil Jackson (b.1945), Scottie Pippen, Dennis Rodman, Luc Longley, and Steve Kerr.

Little Guys Pound Big Homers

In a slugfest that would make Mark McGwire and Sammy Sosa proud, the Little League team from Toms River, New Jersey, out-homered the squad from Kashima, Japan, to win the Little League World Series, 12–9, on August 29 in Williamsport, Pennsylvania. This was the first American team to claim the title since Long Beach, California, won back-to-back championships in 1992 and 1993.

A total of 11 homers highlighted the game, six of them for the New Jersey team. Shortstop Chris Cardone hit a pair in consecutive at-bats—the second one a game-deciding two-run shot in the sixth inning. Tetsuya Furukawa belted three of Kashima's five home runs.

Besides several lead changes, the spirited international contest featured Sayaka Tsushima, the sixth girl to play in a Little League World Series, the first in a final, and the first from a Far East champion. She went 0 for 3.

answer, the 1998 baseball season, hailed as one of the greatest ever, turned out to be a total lovefest.

Every good love story needs powerful characters, and this season had a strong cast. In the individual performance category, Mark McGwire (b.1963) and Sammy Sosa (b.1968) had an epic battle for top honors. Not since Yankees teammates Mickey Mantle and Roger Maris staged a home-run battle in 1961 had a pair of sluggers faced off in such a dynamic duel. (Mantle ended the season with 54 homers, while Maris eclipsed Babe Ruth's record of 60 home runs, hitting number 61 on the last day of the season.)

McGwire, the former Oakland A's slugger now with the St. Louis Cardinals,

had smacked 11 homers by the end of April. Chicago Cubs outfielder Sosa had just six home runs by May 1, but went crazy in June, smacking a major league-record 20. At the All-Star break in July, Sosa had 33 home runs to McGwire's 37.

While that tale unfolded, on the pitcher's mound a precocious Cub and a hefty lefty made fans swoon with a pair of one-day masterpieces. On May 6 at Chicago's Wrigley Field, 20-year-old rookie Kerry Wood struck out 20 Houston Astros in a single game to set a National League record and tie a major league one. On May 17 at Yankee Stadium, veteran left-hander David Wells (b.1963) pitched only the 15th perfect game in Major League Baseball history, retiring all 27 Minnesota Twins he faced in a 4–0 Yankees victory. Renowned for his excess weight and excessive ways off the field, for at least one day everyone focused on Wells' pitching excellence. "You can criticize his weight, his wild lifestyle, his tattoos, or his gruff demeanor, but none of that mattered to the Minnesota Twins on May 17, 1998," wrote James Buckley Jr. in his 2002 book, *Perfect*.

The Yankees, though not quite perfect, came pretty darn close in 1998. With an ideal combination of outstanding pitching, timely hitting, solid defense, and unselfish team chemistry, the Yanks won an American-League record 114 games in the regular season (against just 48 losses). After sweeping the Texas Rangers in the best-of-five-games division playoffs beginning in late September, they eliminated the Cleveland Indians, four games to two, in the American League Championship Series. Saving their best for last, in the World Series in October New York brought down its opponents, the San Diego Padres—by going 4–0. A perfect sweep.

Meanwhile, McGwire and Sosa continued chasing Maris' mythical home run record. Sosa reached the 50 plateau on August 11; McGwire arrived there on the 20th. By the end of the month, when they both stood at 55 homers, Maris' widow and family were graciously and anxiously awaiting baseball history. They sat proudly in box seats at St. Louis' Busch Stadium on September 7 when McGwire tied the record at 61, and were back there the next day when he hit No. 62. Ironically, the record breaker was his shortest home run of the season.

On September 11, at Wrigley Field, Sosa kept pace with homers 61 and 62. He ended up hitting four more to finish at 66, while McGwire kept up his assault on the record books right up until the last day of the season, blasting two to finish with a phenomenal total of 70 home runs.

Other Milestones of 1998

✔ New Year's Day saw the University of Michigan end a 12–0 season with a 21–16 win over Washington State University in the Rose Bowl. Nonetheless, the Michigan Wolverines shared the number one college football ranking with 13–0 University of Nebraska.

✔ In January, CBS, Fox, and ABC/ESPN committed $17.6 billion from 1998 to 2005 to televise NFL games. Color analyst John Madden signed a five-year deal with Fox worth $8 million per year.

✔ A federal magistrate ruled, on February 11, that under the Americans with Disabilities Act, handicapped pro golfer Casey Martin could use a motorized golf cart in PGA tournaments, despite tournament rules to the contrary.

✔ In a labor dispute, NBA team owners imposed a player lockout on June 29 that would eventually shorten the 1998–1999 basketball season.

Ila Borders

✔ On July 9, Ila Borders, who made baseball history in 1995 as the first woman to play for a men's team (Southern California College of Cosa Mesa), became the first female pitcher to start a minor league game. The 24-year-old lefty pitched five innings for the Duluth-Superior Dukes in their 8–3 loss to the Sioux Falls Canaries in the Northern League.

✔ Baltimore Orioles shortstop Cal Ripken ended his streak of consecutive games played at 2,632 on September 20 at Camden Yards. Ripken took himself out of the lineup.

✔ On November 16, Toronto Blue Jays pitcher Roger Clemens, on the strength of his 20–6 record, 2.65 ERA, and 271 strikeouts, won an unprecedented fifth Cy Young Award, given to the best pitcher of the season.

1999

Money Players

On January 6, the Baseball Writers' Association of America (BBWAA) elected three first-time candidates into the National Baseball Hall of Fame in Cooperstown, New York: Nolan Ryan, George Brett, and Robin Yount (players are currently eligible for induction five years after they retire). The last time that happened was in 1936, and those players—Ty Cobb, Walter Johnson, Christy Mathewson, Babe Ruth, and Honus Wagner—were in the very first group of baseball players enshrined in the Hall of Fame.

The news brought cheers from baseball fans who appreciated the remarkable achievements of each player, although it particularly heartened sports collectors. For as much as money drove athletes, team owners, television networks, and corporate sponsors during the 1990s, the memorabilia and collectibles industry shifted into high gear during the decade, too. Values of trading cards and autographed items—from game-used jerseys to canceled paychecks—skyrocketed.

The financial significance of the Hall of Fame announcement was the instant increase in price of items related to Ryan, Brett, and Yount. Getting into the Hall raises a player's stature, and therefore the worth of his likeness and things connected to him. For example, Ryan's rookie card (1968 Topps #177) rose from about $1,000 to nearly $3,000, practically overnight.

Proof of just how crazy the market had gotten surfaced on January 12, when the baseball that Mark McGwire hit for his historic 70th home run in 1998 sold at auction for slightly more than $3 million. A couple of weeks later, the buyer revealed himself: Todd McFarlane, the creator of *Spawn* and other superhero comic books and toys. In fact, the owner of the so-called McFarlane Collection had plunked down another $300,000 or so to acquire McGwire's No. 1, 63, 67, 68, 69, and 70 home-run balls, along with Sammy Sosa's No. 33, 61, and 66. (In 2003, he paid $450,000 for the 71st home run ball hit by Barry Bonds in setting a new single-season record.)

While you chew on that, consider Karen Shemonsky of Clarks Summit, Pennsylvania, who paid $7,475 for Cobb's false teeth—honestly—at a Sotheby's baseball memorabilia auction on September 27. "[Friends] keep calling me,

World Class *The U.S. women's soccer team proved to be the best in the world in 1999 (page 88).*

saying, 'Why would you want that?'" Shemonsky told reporters. "My sister goes on cruises. I'd rather have this in my hand." Biting commentary on the times, for sure.

Every Dog Deserves His Day

In the 1990s, the University of Connecticut Huskies were heralded from Juneau to Jupiter (Florida) for their outstanding basketball. UConn's men's program, since the arrival in 1986 of head coach Jim Calhoun, rose from the doghouse to the penthouse in the Big East Conference. And coach Geno Auriemma, guided the Lady Huskies to national prominence with a perfect season and a national championship in 1995.

It took four years for Calhoun's men to catch up, but they finally won it all in 1999, downing Duke University in the NCAA championship game, 77–74, on March 29 at Tropicana Field in St. Petersburg, Florida. Coming into the tournament, UConn held the unenviable record for most NCAA appearances (20) without reaching the Final Four. What made this championship even sweeter was vanquishing the Blue Devils, who

Two Out of Three Ain't Bad *Jockey Chris Antley rode Charismatic (6) to victory in the Kentucky Derby and the Preakness Stakes, but fell short of the coveted Triple Crown in the Belmont Stakes.*

had become UConn's nemesis in recent years. Seven times during the 1990s, UConn had played into the Sweet 16, and each time they'd fallen short—twice to Duke. The most devastating defeat was in the 1990 tournament, when Christian Laettner's last-second shot sent UConn home.

Duke, with only one loss all season and an immaculate 16–0 record in the tough Atlantic Coast Conference, was heavily favored. Yet UConn, with a 28–2 regular-season record, didn't exactly fit the underdog profile. Sure enough, coach Mike Krzyzewski's Blue Devils, powered by 6-foot-8, 260-pound forward Elton Brand—the national player of the year—couldn't stop the sharp shooting of UConn guard Richard "Rip" Hamilton, who went

on a game-high 27-point tear. Shortly after Duke's Trajan Langdon was called for traveling while driving to score the potential game-winning basket, the Huskies fell into a celebratory dog pile on the court.

Charismatic, but Not Charmed

It had been 21 years since thoroughbred horse racing celebrated a Triple Crown winner. Affirmed, in 1978, was the last horse to capture the Kentucky Derby, the Preakness Stakes, and the Belmont Stakes in the same year. In 1997 and 1998, Silver Charm and Real Quiet, respectively, came oh-so close, winning the first two legs, then finishing second in the Belmont.

This year, the 125th running of the Kentucky Derby at Churchill Downs in Louisville on May 1 was won by Charismatic, ridden by jockey Chris Antley. It marked the fourth Derby victory for trainer D. Wayne Lukas and his third in the 1990s. Two Saturdays later, on May 15 at Pimlico Race Course in Baltimore, Antley and the three-year-old chestnut horse crossed the finish line first again, passing two contenders on the final turn. "I think we can win it," Lukas said to reporters afterward, anxiously anticipating the Belmont Stakes in three weeks.

Charismatic came out of the gate fast and strong on June 5 at Belmont Park in Elmont, New York, enticing a crowd of 85,818 (the biggest in New York racing history) to believe the Triple Crown was possible. He remained in the lead until about an eighth of a mile was left on the mile-and-a-half racetrack, when a long-shot, Lemon Drop Kid, passed him. Vision and Verse, another longshot, also over-took Charismatic, who finished third.

In gallantly battling back, Charismatic fractured two bones in his lower left foreleg (an area comparable to the human ankle). He had successful surgery the next day, but his racing days were over.

Won for the Good Guys

The NBA almost didn't happen this year. In the latest round of an ongoing struggle between owners seeking to control costs and players seeking to maximize their salaries, the first three months of the NBA season were canceled. Without a contract between owners and players, owners locked out the players while negotiations went on between the two sides. The entire preseason and all games through mid-January were canceled. Finally, to fans' relief, the season began on February 2.

The second edition of the Bulls-without-Jordan NBA Finals (after a shortened regular season of 50 games instead of 82) was a Good Guys versus Bad Guys showdown in June, pitting the angelic San Antonio Spurs against the devilish New York Knicks. The typecasting was a no-brainer, with gentle giants David Robinson and Tim Duncan set to slay New York's surly Marcus Camby and coach-choking Latrell Sprewell (see page 72).

In the end, the Spurs smote the Knicks in five games to gain their first championship in the team's 26-year history. The lopsided outcome, however, had more to do with New York's offensive ineptitude and inability to stop San Antonio's twin seven-foot towers than any clash of virtues. After the title-clincher in New York on June 25, in which Finals MVP Duncan scored 31 points in the 78–77 San Antonio victory, Spurs head coach Gregg Popovich told Knicks head coach Jeff Van Gundy, "I've got Tim and you don't. That's the difference."

When Dallas Froze Over

Until the 1990s, NHL teams had been located almost exclusively in cold-weather cities, with the exception of the Los Angeles Kings. Then ice-challenged places such as Miami, Atlanta, Phoenix, and Dallas landed teams. On June 19 at the Marine Midland Arena in Buffalo, the Dallas Stars—which relocated from Minneapolis, Minnesota, in 1993—became the first Sun Belt team to hoist the Stanley Cup.

It took some effort to lift it over their heads. In game six of the best-of-seven series, the Stars, up three games to two, played the Buffalo Sabres to a 1–1 tie in regulation and two overtime periods. At 14:51 of the third overtime, Dallas rightwinger Brett Hull scored the winning goal. Or did he? Replays seemed to show that his left skate was illegally in the goal crease before he shot, which would have voided the goal. Despite the Sabres' strong protest, NHL officials let it stand. It went down in the record books as the second-longest overtime game in the history of the Stanley Cup finals, the longest to decide a winner—and, unofficially, the most controversial.

1999

Their World Cup Runneth Overtime

On July 10, a crowd of 90,185 at the Rose Bowl in Pasadena, California—the largest ever to watch a women's sporting event anywhere—witnessed the United States outduel China in a thrilling penalty-kick shootout to win the 1999 Women's World Cup soccer tournament. The shootout followed a 0–0 tie after 90 minutes of regulation play and a scoreless 30-minute overtime. United States defender Brandi Chastain blasted the winning shot past Chinese goalkeeper Gao Hong to break a 4–4 deadlock.

The U.S. national team had made history in 1991 by winning the first women's World Cup, and had taken the gold medal in the inaugural Olympic women's soccer tournament at the 1996 Summer Games in Atlanta. Still, the sport and the team played in relative obscurity beyond those high-profile events. World Cup '99, though—perhaps sparked by the popular success of the men's World Cup held in the United States in 1994 and growing interest in professional Major League Soccer—drew record crowds over its three-week, seven-city tournament, held June 19 to July 10.

The American women steamrolled through the first round, outscoring their three opponents 13–1. In the quarterfinals, they outlasted Germany, 3–2, then shut out Brazil, 2–0, to advance to the finals against their archrivals.

The United States had beaten China in both the 1991 World Cup and the 1996 Olympic championship games. This final turned into a grueling stalemate. It boiled down to the final shootout, during which five players from each team alternate shots on goal from 12 yards out. After China tied it at 3–3, American star Mia Hamm—goalless in her last four games—nailed a pressure-packed kick. China answered, and then came 30-year-old Chastain's date with soccer immortality. When the Rose Bowl exploded with cheers, Chastain dropped to her knees and pulled off one of the more memorable celebrations ever. She ripped off her jersey to reveal a sports bra. The image of Chastain excitedly ripping off her jersey, as the men have long done in soccer, became an icon for tough, exuberant female athletes all over the world.

That wasn't the end of this heroic championship squad. With national attention focused on them, the eight-team Women's United Soccer Association (WUSA) professional league was formed, and all 20 of the '99 Cup players signed on, along with a roster of premier international stars. WUSA launched on April 14, 2001, with Chastain's Bay Area Cyber-Rays facing off against Hamm's Washington Freedom at Robert F. Kennedy Stadium in Washington, D.C. The Freedom defeated the CyberRays, 1–0.

Extra-Shimmery All-Star Game

Major League Baseball's annual All-Star Game is traditionally a midseason break, where the game's top players shine for a couple of innings apiece to the fans' delight. The 1999 edition, however, played under the lights on July 13 at Boston's vintage Fenway Park, turned into an especially lustrous affair. Along with some sparkling individual performances, the sport itself put on a spectacular show.

As the last All-Star Game of the 20th century, MLB used the occasion to announce the nominees for its All-Century Team in an emotional pre-game ceremony. Onto the diamond trotted such living legends as outfielders Hank Aaron, Stan Musial, and Willie Mays, pitchers Bob Feller, Juan Marichal, Bob Gibson, and Sandy Koufax, and catchers Johnny Bench and Yogi Berra.

The loudest ovation, however, was saved for Ted Williams (1918–2002). Williams played for Boston from 1939 to 1960 and retired in 1960 with 521 home runs and a career .344 average. He earned a reputation as the greatest hitter who ever lived. However, the gruff and uncompromising Hall of Famer actually had not always been a fan favorite during his playing days in Boston.

For this night, though, the 80-year-old Williams, known as "the Splendid Splinter," was universally beloved—by the capacity crowd of 34,187, his fellow All-Century candidates, and the game's all-stars. Two strokes and a broken hip in recent years forced Williams to take the field in a golf cart, which he rode around Fenway to thunderous applause. He climbed out near the pitcher's mound, and, after tossing the ceremonial first pitch, was spontaneously surrounded by players past and present. "There was a baseball love-in on the mound," wrote the Associated Press the next day. "The stars of the night and the stars of the century swamping Ted Williams, gazing at

How Sweep It Is

Following the events at the All-Star Game, baseball fell into its predictable pattern. After winning their respective divisions, the New York Yankees and Atlanta Braves powered through two rounds of the playoffs to meet in the World Series, October 23 to 27. It was billed as a showdown to decide not just the best team of the year, but also of the decade. Although the Braves had only captured one World Series since 1990 (defeating the Cleveland Indians in 1997), compared to two for the Yankees (1996 versus Atlanta, 1998 versus the San Diego Padres), the Braves had dominated the National League, winning eight division titles and five league championships.

It didn't turn out to be much of a battle. But for a lone defeat at the right arm of eventual A.L. Cy Young Award winner Pedro Martinez in game three of the A.L. Championship Series, the Yankees went undefeated in the entire postseason, winning 11 of 12 games. In sweeping the Braves in four straight games, the Yankees starting pitchers only gave up seven earned runs and held opposing batters to a paltry .200 average. New York relief pitcher and Series MVP Mariano Rivera pitched 4 2/3 innings, earned two saves, and registered an unblemished earned run average of 0.00.

him in awe, reaching over each other to shake his hand."

The game got off to a sizzling start when hometown Red Sox pitcher Pedro Martinez struck out all three batters in the first inning—an All-Star Game record—and then two batters in the second, including St. Louis' home run king, Mark McGwire. Martinez's two stellar innings earned him the game's Most Valuable Player award. Then, with Cal Ripken Jr. and a trio of Cleveland Indians (Kenny Lofton, Manny Ramirez, and Roberto Alomar) each driving in a run, the American League beat the National League, 4–1.

1999

It's About the Bike

Among the most grueling competitions in sports is the annual Tour de France bicycle race. Even for a world-class athlete in peak condition, biking 2,287 miles around France over 20 days may be the ultimate physical and mental challenge. Now imagine doing it after surviving a near-fatal bout with cancer.

Meet Lance Armstrong. By winning the 1999 Tour de France on July 25, the 27-year-old Texan did more than conquer the brutal course and 179 of the world's top cyclists. He beat death. In October 1996, he was diagnosed with testicular cancer, which rapidly spread throughout his body, including to his lungs and brain. When asked to calculate Armstrong's odds of survival, the doctor said candidly,

"Almost none." After two operations to remove golf ball-sized tumors and extensive chemotherapy, Armstrong launched his courageous comeback early in 1998.

He had shown flashes of brilliance in his racing career, winning the one-day World Championship in 1993 and individual stages of the Tour in 1993 and 1995. Yet his poor showings in the Tour's exhausting mountain climbs had denied Armstrong the chance to join Greg LeMond as the only other American to win cycling's most prestigious event. This year, fueled by the same indomitable spirit it took to overcome his lethal disease, Armstrong annihilated the mountain stages.

Riding with the U.S. Postal Service team, Armstrong won the 86th Tour's opening sprint, which allowed him to begin the race wearing the overall leader's yellow jersey. He lost it, then regained it for good in the eighth stage. He attacked the Alps and Pyrenees with such undaunted strength that the French media wondered if he was using banned performance-enhancing drugs. Armstrong overcame those obstacles, too, when race officials cleared him of any wrongdoing.

By the start of the 20th and final stage, Armstrong held an insurmountable lead of 6:19 minutes over his closest competitor. Resplendent in the yellow jersey, he pedaled triumphantly down Paris' famed Champs Elysee to the finish line, 7:37 ahead of Switzerland's Alex Zuelle. Besides winning four stages, including the toughest of the long mountain stages, Armstrong claimed a victory for cancer survivors everywhere. (See page 98 for more.)

Sister, Sister *The Williams sisters (Serena, left, and Venus) became the dominant players in women's tennis at the turn of the century. They teamed to win the U.S. Open doubles title in 1999.*

Other Milestones of 1999

✔ The University of Tennessee won the Fiesta Bowl on January 4, beating Florida State University, 23–16, to gain its first national championship in 47 years. It was the first national title game played as part of the new Bowl Championship Series (see page 77), which took effect in the 1998 college season.

✔ The Denver Broncos repeated as Super Bowl champs on January 31 at Pro Player Stadium in Miami, where John Elway threw for 336 yards against the Atlanta Falcons in a 34–19 Denver victory.

✔ On March 4 in San Jose, the top-ranked Purdue University women's basketball team defeated Duke, 62–45, to claim its first NCAA national title.

✔ At a track and field meet in Athens, Greece, on June 16, Maurice Greene ran the 100-meter sprint in a world record time of 9.79 seconds.

✔ New York Yankees pitcher David Cone recorded the 16th perfect game in Major League baseball history on July 18, shutting out the Montreal Expos, 6–0, at Yankee Stadium.

David Cone celebrates with Joe Girardi

✔ On August 7, a day after baseball star Tony Gwynn of the San Diego Padres collected his 3,000th career hit, Wade Boggs, then with the Tampa Bay Devil Rays, became the first to reach the mark with a home run.

✔ CBS renewed its broadcast rights to the NCAA men's basketball tournament on November 18 by signing a $6-billion, 11-year contract.

Sister Act

While other fathers in his Los Angeles neighborhood were taking their daughters to birthday parties or ballet lessons, Richard Williams watched his two little girls hit tennis balls to each other. Venus (b.1980) and her sister Serena (b. 1981), younger by 15 months, began playing tennis at age four and entered their first tournament when they were nine and eight.

The Williams sisters were 18 and 17 in 1999. They'd both turned pro and had quickly risen in the Women's Tennis Association's world rankings. In September, at the U.S. Open in Flushing, New York, Serena ruled the day.

Seeded seventh in the tournament, she engineered several upsets en route to her first career Grand Slam singles title. Serena not only became the lowest seed to win the women's title in the Open Era (since 1968) but also the second African-American woman ever (after Althea Gibson [b. 1927]) to win a Grand Slam singles title. A day later, she and big sis captured the Open doubles title. The two went on to dominate women's tennis into the new millennium.

2000–2003

Sports in America continues to grow in both size and importance. This chapter highlights some of the more recent events and issues in the sports world. As the first decade of the 21st century moves on, these may be the topics worth keeping an eye on.

Everyone's Chasing Tiger

Tiger Woods kept proving why he is the real deal. Make that unreal. He continued to dominate the PGA Tour into the new millennium, as his impact on the sport reached the status of baseball giant Babe Ruth. Other gifted golfers, such as Ernie Els, Phil Mickelson, David Duval, Jim Furyk, and Sergio Garcia, mounted valiant challenges, yet Tiger vanquished most to remain the top-ranked player in the world. Winning tournaments by ridiculous margins, drawing unprecedented galleries and TV ratings, and lifting his game to ever-loftier levels, Woods gained further consideration as perhaps the best golfer ever.

Look no further than the year 2000. On June 18 at Pebble Beach, California, he captured his first U.S. Open and third major tournament in record-setting fashion. His 15-stroke victory was the largest winning margin ever in a major. Just 35 days later, on July 23, he wrapped up a 19-under-par performance on the Old Course at St. Andrews, Scotland—the esteemed birthplace of golf—to clinch the British Open. With that, Tiger, at age 24, became the youngest golfer to have won all four majors; the great Jack Nicklaus was two years older when he achieved his career Grand Slam.

Then, on August 20, down by two strokes to Bob May early in the final round of the PGA Championship at Valhalla Golf Club in Louisville, Kentucky, Tiger birdied the last two holes of regulation to force a three-hole playoff. A birdie and two pars later, he had his third major of the year, a feat last accomplished by Ben Hogan (1912–1997) in 1953. "Someday I'll tell my grandkids I played in the same tournament as Tiger Woods," marveled Hall of Famer Tom Watson (b.1949). "We are witnessing a phenomenon here that the game may never, ever see again."

They saw the phenom again all too soon, at the 2001 Masters in Augusta, Georgia. On April 8, playing the final round with Duval and Mickelson on his tail, Tiger maintained his steely focus and

The Drive for Five *After defeating cancer, Lance Armstrong defeated the world's best cyclists to win his fifth Tour de France in 2003 (page 98).*

held on to win by two strokes. In so doing, he became the first golfer to hold all four major tournament titles at the same time.

Woods' majors streak ended there, but he started a new one in 2002. He defended his Masters title on April 14, followed by another U.S. Open triumph on June 16 at Bethpage State Park on Long Island, New York—the first time the tournament was held on a public venue. He

Women Golfers Roar, Too

Annika Sorenstam (b.1970) emerged as the top woman golfer around the turn of the century, ranking number one on the tour five times from 1995 to 2002. The Swedish native enjoyed a phenomenal 2001, with eight wins, six second-place finishes, and 20 top-10 finishes in cruising to her fourth career Player of the Year award. She raised the bar even higher in 2002, joining Mickey Wright as the only other player to win 11 tournaments in a season (Wright won 11 times in 1964; she also won an LPGA-record 13 tournaments in 1963).

Then came 2003, which proved a watershed year, not only for Sorenstam, but pros of both genders. Before Sorenstam made history by becoming the first woman to play in a PGA tournament since Babe Didrikson Zaharias (1911–1956) in 1945, a more pivotal battle of the sexes was waged at the Masters in April. The opening salvo was fired in June 2002 when Martha Burk, head of the National Council of Women's Organizations, sent a letter to Augusta National Golf Club chairman William "Hootie" Johnson, urging that the men-only club admit women members for the first time in its 70-year history. Johnson steadfastly refused, and a heated national debate ensued. The basic issue: women's rights to equal access versus a private club's right to control its membership.

The controversy came to a head—sort of—on day three of the tournament. Burk led a smaller-than-expected group of protesters outside the club, while a handful of Hootie supporters, curious onlookers, and a CBS television audience (watching the tournament commercial-free after Johnson voided sponsorships) looked on. In the end, Augusta remained all-male and Burk vowed to resume her campaign. This is one issue that is sure to be raised again in the future.

For her part, at the Bank of America Colonial tournament in Fort Worth, Texas, in May, Sorenstam missed the cut (eligibility to compete in the final two days of a four-day tournament) by four strokes after rounds of 71 and 74. However, her play earned mostly raves from fans and the media.

In December, Sorenstam set a record in the invite-only Skins Game by winning $175,000 on the first day of the two-day competition. Sorenstam was the first woman asked to play in the 19-year-old event, in which golfers play head to head for prize money offered on each hole.

Her two-day Skins Game total of $225,000 capped off a remarkable year for both her personally and for women in golf.

In early 2004, 14-year-old Michelle Wie made more history as the youngest golfer in a pro event. She played the first two rounds of the Sony Open in Hawaii, stunning onlookers with her precocious talent and barely missing the cut.

Annika Sorenstam

won a total of five PGA Tour events in 2002, earning his fourth consecutive Player of the Year Award from the Golf Writers Association of America.

Incredibly, after failing to win the 2003 Masters and U.S. Open, there was talk of a slump. It quickly died down in early July after he blistered the field at the 100th Western Open at Cog Hill Country Club near Chicago. After matching the course record with an opening-round nine-under-par 63, he never trailed. Woods followed with rounds of 70–65–69 to finish at 21-under 267—five shots better than runner-up Rich Beem. "I was never in [a slump]," Tiger said. "I told you guys it was just a matter of being patient." And being a remarkably talented athlete.

All the while, Venus insisted that Serena was closing in. Sure enough, in 2002, the sisters met in three consecutive Grand Slam finals—the French Open, Wimbledon, and the U.S. Open—with Serena winning all three. She ended the season as the top-ranked player in the world, with Venus second.

It was another all-Williams final at the 2003 Australian Open, where the sisters became the first duo to reach four straight Grand Slam finals in the Open Era—and where Serena won her fourth in a row. "I wish I could have been the winner," said an emotional, yet gracious Venus after the deciding match, "but of course you have a great champion in Serena." No doubt, this sibling rivalry is far from over.

Out of This Williams World

After landing on the WTA Tour scene in the late 1990s, the Williams sisters, Serena and Venus, ruled the early part of the next decade, especially on the prestigious Grand Slam circuit. In 2000, Venus defeated her younger sister in the semifinals at Wimbledon en route to her first Grand Slam title, topping reigning champion Lindsay Davenport. Venus beat Davenport again in the U.S. Open final, then capped off a sensational year with the singles crown at the Summer Olympic Games in Sydney—where she and Serena also collected the doubles gold medal.

Venus defended her Wimbledon and U.S. Open titles in 2001. At the Open, she and Serena became the first sisters to meet in a Grand Slam final since Wimbledon in 1884.

Despite Tarnish, Two Olympics Shine

Scandal rocked the Olympic movement in November 1998 when it was alleged that International Olympic Committee members had been bribed by Salt Lake City, Utah, officials to influence the city's selection as the site for the 2002 Winter Games. An investigation prompted the resignations of two top Salt Lake Olympic Organizing Committee executives and several IOC members, as well as sweeping reforms throughout the IOC, based in Lausanne, Switzerland. (In early 2004, a Utah judge threw out the case against the U.S. official who was charged, citing lack of evidence. However, the IOC reforms remained in place.)

No Olympic athletes were implicated in the mess, so when the 2000 Summer Games opened in Sydney on September

World's Fastest Woman *Sprinter Marion Jones is all smiles as she shows off one of her medals—she won three golds and two bronze—at the 2000 Summer Olympics in Sydney, Australia.*

15, the focus was on competition, not controversy. Americans brought home the most medals—39 gold, 25 silver, 33 bronze—while turning in a number of memorable performances. Many came in swimming , which featured 13 new world records and a much-anticipated showdown between the U.S. and Australian teams. The United States outshined its Aussie hosts, 14 golds to five.

Sprinting sensation Marion Jones (b.1975) may have failed in her well-publicized quest to become the first American to win five track and field gold medals at one Olympics, but three gold medals, plus two bronze medals, were more than impressive. She and teammate Maurice Greene claimed the title of "world's fastest humans" by winning their respective 100-meter races.

The Olympic spirit celebrates underdogs, and there was none more lionized in Sydney than U.S. Greco-Roman wrestler Rulon Gardner. With no major title to his name, the hulking Wyoming native upset legendary Russian Alexander "The Beast" Karelin, who hadn't lost a match in 13 years. Nearly as stunning was the 4–0 upset victory by the American baseball team over the heavily favored Cubans in the championship game.

The IOC storm had subsided by the time the 2002 Winter Games convened in Salt Lake City on February 8, but then a different type of international tempest brewed—around the pairs figure skating event. Soon after Russians Elena Berezhnaya and Anton Sikharulidze narrowly won the gold medal over a seemingly superior duo from Canada, David Pelletier and Jamie Sale, a judging scandal erupted. It was quickly determined that the French judge's vote had been biased—she had allegedly agreed to vote the Russians up in exchange for another judge's vote for a French pair—and an unprecedented second set of golds was awarded to the Canadians six days later.

Although shocking, at least the women's figure skating results weren't contested. Michelle Kwan (b.1980), the holder of four world and six U.S. titles and silver medalist at the 1998 Games in Nagano, Japan, was expected to finally mine the Olympic gold. But just as teenager Tara Lipinski skated away with it in Nagano, this time another American teen, 16-year-old Sarah Hughes from Great Neck, New York, leap-frogged from fourth place after the short program to swipe the gold.

A bittersweet victory was claimed by Jim Shea in the men's skeleton event, which hadn't been in the Olympics since 1948. After sliding face down on a sleek fiberglass sled along the curvy bobsled track at 80 miles per hour, a triumphant Shea held up a picture of his grandfather to the television cameras. Jack Shea, who won two gold medals in speedskating at the 1932 Olympics in Lake Placid, New York, had died just a few weeks earlier at the age of 91. But his son, Jim Sr.—a cross-country skiing competitor at the 1964 Games in Innsbruck, Austria—was in Salt Lake to congratulate the youngest member of America's first three-generation family of Winter Olympians.

Baseball Survives No-Win Situation

Bad memories of the long, bitter strike by Major League Baseball players in 1994, which cancelled that year's playoffs and World Series, resurfaced as another work stoppage threatened to wreck the 2002 season. Luckily, the players and owners agreed on a new collective bargaining agreement just hours before the August 31 deadline.

Then, on July 9 at Miller Park in Milwaukee, Commissioner Bud Selig decided to call the All-Star Game a tie at 7–7 after 11 innings, when both teams ran out of pitchers. Fans were outraged. MLB

The Day the Earth Stood Still

September 11, 2001, will forever be remembered as the day when life in America underwent a dramatic and deadly change. Early that sunny morning, a horrible terrorist plot unfolded. Two commercial airplanes loaded with passengers were hijacked and deliberately slammed into the twin towers at New York City's World Trade Center. The towers collapsed shortly thereafter. At about the same time, a third hijacked plane was flown into the Pentagon in Washington, D.C. A fourth plane, reportedly targeted for the U.S. Capitol building, crashed in a field in Pennsylvania after passengers overpowered the hijackers. In total, more than 3,000 people were killed.

As a shocked nation mourned, everyday activities came to a virtual standstill. Cancellations in the sports world included baseball games for six days, a week of

NFL and college football games, NASCAR, golf, and other major events. "At a certain point," said NFL commissioner Paul Tagliabue, "playing our games can contribute to the healing process. Just not at this time." When the action did resume, special homage was paid to the victims at venues nationwide, and strict new security measures were instituted.

Responsibility for the attacks was claimed by members of the Al Qaeda terrorist network, based largely in Afghanistan and led by Osama bin Laden. On October 7, sports broadcasts were interrupted as President George W. Bush announced the beginning of Operation Enduring Freedom, an American-led military action in Afghanistan to overthrow the Taliban government, which supported Al Qaeda's efforts, and to destroy terrorist operations in the country.

2000–2003

reacted by declaring that the winner of the 2003 Midsummer Classic—played at U.S. Cellular Field, home of the Chicago White Sox—would determine home field advantage for the 2003 World Series (the advantage previously alternated between leagues each year). It looked like the National League had it, until the bottom of the eighth inning when Texas Rangers third baseman Hank Blalock, in his first All-Star at bat, smacked a two-out, two-run, pinch-hit homer off Los Angeles Dodgers closing pitcher Greg Gagne. The Junior Circuit (a.k.a. American League) prevailed, 7–6, when it counted most.

Tour de Lance

As Lance Armstrong took his ceremonial ride along the Champs-Elysees in Paris on July 27, 2003, and crossed the finish line after the 20th and final stage of the world's toughest and most celebrated bicycle race, he joined a very exclusive club. Wearing the leader's yellow jersey, the 31-year-old Texan, racing for the U.S. Postal Service team, had just won his fifth Tour de France. Only four others in the 90 Tours run to that point had won as many (the event was first held in 1903, but was interrupted during both World Wars). Adding to the grandeur of the moment, Armstrong became just the second rider to claim five Tours in a row, joining Spain's Miguel Indurain (b.1964), who dominated from 1991 to 1995. "It's a dream, really a dream," Armstrong said in French from the winner's podium.

All five of Armstrong's victories have been remarkable—they came after a near-fatal fight with cancer in 1996—but this one took on mythical proportions. He suffered through a stomach flu just before the three-week, 2,130-mile race began on July 5; he survived bumps and bruises from two crashes; he narrowly avoided a potentially disastrous spill in the mountains. Plus, the competition had never been so tight. Armstrong finished a scant 61 seconds ahead of five-time runner-up Jan Ullrich of Germany, whose hopes had tumbled along with his bike on a rain-soaked road during a crucial time trial the day before. Armstrong's previous margins of victory had all been more than six minutes. "I think this year I had to rely more on strategy than on physical gifts or physical fitness," he stated.

Armstrong pledged to be back in 2004. "I love cycling, I love my job, and I will be back for a sixth," he said.

The Newcomers' Club

Call it coincidence, luck, or a universal leveling of playing fields, but the number of teams winning their first championships as the curtain rose on the new century was unprecedented. Start with the NFL. From Super Bowl XI in 1977, the year the Oakland Raiders won their first, until Super Bowl XXXII in 1998, when the Denver Broncos at last claimed the Lombardi Trophy, only four teams became first-time champions. Then, following a Broncos' repeat in 1999, came a run of four such teams.

The St. Louis Rams stopped the Tennessee Titans at the one-yard line to preserve a 23–16 victory in Super Bowl XXXIV on January 30, 2000. A year later, the Baltimore Ravens used a rock 'em, sock 'em defense to belittle the New York Giants, 34–7. Next, the sure right foot of place kicker Adam Vinatieri, whose 48-yard field goal as time expired (the only Super Bowl to be won on the final play) nipped the Rams, 20–17, and booted the New England Patriots onto the Super Bowl winners' list. Finally, on January 25, 2003, the Tampa Bay Buccaneers, with a 48–21 upset of the Raiders, joined the pantheon.

Baseball added two new teams to its roster of World Series champions. On November 4, 2001, a bloop single by the Arizona Diamondbacks' Luis Gonzalez on a pitch from New York Yankees closer Mariano Rivera in the bottom of the ninth inning of game seven in Phoenix, gave the Diamondbacks their first title. The Anaheim Angels got their first championship in a grand finale, too, on October 27, 2002. Game seven of the World Series against Barry Bonds and the San Francisco Giants went to the host Angels, 4–1.

With the growing trend in underclassmen leaving men's college basketball for the NBA before graduating, more schools had a chance to grab that brass ring. The University of Maryland reached its first Final Four in 2001, but lost to Michigan State. The Terrapins made it back in 2002, fending off a feisty squad from the University of Indiana, 64–52, on April 1 at the Georgia Dome in Atlanta. On April 7, 2003, the Orangemen of Syracuse University—appearing in the final game for the third time since 1987—outlasted the University of Kansas, 81–78, to gain their first NCAA title.

And then there was the first-time winner of the first-time sport that never

had a second chance. The XFL, an eight-team pro football league created by World Wrestling Federation founder Vince McMahon, launched on February 3, 2001. On April 21, the Los Angeles Xtreme dominated the San Francisco Demons, 38–6, at the L.A. Coliseum in the so-called Million Dollar Game to become the one and only XFL champion. McMahon announced on May 10 that the league was folding after just one season.

The Police Blotter Spreads

Athletes' run-ins with the law can probably be traced all the way back to some ancient Greek chariot racer swiping a set of wheelrims off a rival's ride. By the 20th century, the offenses ranged from

Real-Life Drama *Los Angeles Lakers basketball superstar Kobe Bryant and his wife, Vanessa, face the media after Bryant was accused of raping a woman at a resort in Eagle, Colorado.*

2000–2003

barroom brawls to gambling on games. In the 1990s, however, as players' salaries and off-the-field temptations escalated, so did the related crimes.

Former running back O.J. Simpson was acquitted of killing his wife and her friend (but found liable in a civil suit), heavyweight champion Mike Tyson went to prison for rape, Dallas Cowboys receiver Michael Irvin got busted for possession of cocaine, and the rap sheet on baseball's Darryl Strawberry included hitting his wife, soliciting a prostitute, and income-tax evasion.

In the 2000s, things got even worse. Among the more notorious cases early in the decade:

- Former Carolina Panthers NFL receiver Rae Carruth was convicted in January 2001 of conspiracy stemming from the fatal drive-by shooting of his pregnant girlfriend, Cherica Adams, in November 1999. He was sentenced to serve at least 18 years, 11 months in jail.

- In February 2001, star NBA rebounder turned broadcaster Jayson Williams was indicted on a charge of aggravated manslaughter in connection with the shooting death of his limousine driver inside Williams' New Jersey mansion. He pleaded not guilty and was awaiting trial at press time.

- No one will ever know all the facts related to the July 2002 disappearance at sea and suspected murder of former NBA player Bison Dele (a.k.a. Brian Williams) after his brother, Miles Dabord—the FBI's prime suspect—mysteriously died in Mexico several weeks later.

- Baylor University basketball player Patrick Dennehy was reported missing on June 19, 2003, and foul play was immediately suspected. In late July, two days after friend and teammate Carlton Dotson was arrested and charged with Dennehy's murder, the body was found in Waco, Texas.

- On July 4, 2003, officials in Eagle County, Colorado, arrested Los Angeles Lakers superstar Kobe Bryant, 24, on suspicion of sexually assaulting a 19-year-old woman who worked at a resort where Bryant was staying. On July 18, he was formally charged, and in an emotional press conference later that day admitted to having consensual sex with his accuser. Bryant's very public image—as a clean-cut member of the three-time NBA champion Lakers and a highly paid pitchman for McDonald's, Coca-Cola, and Nike—fueled a major media circus, as well as the ongoing debate over the role and treatment of athletes in society.

"It seems naive in the extreme to profess amazement that a professional athlete might have extramarital sex, given the privileges of the lifestyle, the ease with which the stars attract women, and the fact that so many high-profile males (a president [referring to President Bill Clinton], for one) have been unfaithful," wrote Jack McCallum in a *Sports Illustrated* cover story the following week. "While some who never bought into Bryant's squeaky-clean persona were still surprised by the allegation of violence, others have long believed he has a darker side. The excavation of his life and character has begun."

Taking It to the 'Net

Sports media and fandom began to change in the 1990s with the advent of the personal computer and the Internet. By 2003, virtually every major and minor sport, league, team, and player was represented on multiple Web sites loaded with news, statistics, photos, video clips, history, and everything else ravenous visitors could digest. Fans also gobbled up Web versions of brand names such as ESPN.com and SportsIllustrated.com, as well as online editions of niche sports media. You name it—lacrosse, Olympics, water polo, horse racing, snowboarding, kite surfing, soccer, bass fishing, *ad infinitum*—you could find it somewhere on the Internet.

The majority of U.S. homes had access to the Internet by then, putting the medium on the verge of replacing newspapers, magazines, and even television as the primary source of sports news and entertainment. High-speed access, via DSL lines or cable modems, promised infinite options for online fans.

Curses, Foiled Again!

With even casual baseball fans eagerly anticipating the match-up and network television executives salivating over the possibilities, the American League Boston Red Sox and the National League Chicago Cubs appeared destined to both break decades of frustration and disappointment and meet in the World Series in 2003.

Alas, each club's historic curse reared its ugly head at just about the last, and

Net Game *ESPN (above)—and just about every other sport, league, team, and media outlet—reaches out to fans via the World Wide Web.*

worst, possible moment—in each league's respective championship series—and the dream World Series never materialized. Instead, the upstart Florida Marlins flouted tradition by whipping the 26-time-champion New York Yankees in six games in the World Series in October. The finale was a five-hit, 2–0 gem by 23-year-old Florida righthander Josh Beckett.

Boston ended 2003 still trying to shake the Curse of the Bambino: Not long after winning the World Series in 1918, the club sold Babe Ruth to the Yankees and hasn't won a Fall Classic since.

The Red Sox were on the verge of returning to baseball's premier stage for the first time since 1986 when they took a 5–2 lead into the bottom of the eighth inning behind pitching ace Pedro Martinez in game seven of the A.L. Championship

2000-2003

Series (ALCS) at Yankee Stadium. But the Yankees rallied to tie the game, then went on to win in the 11th inning on Aaron Boone's solo home run.

Over in the National League, the Cubs haven't won a World Series championship since 1908 or even a league pennant since the 1945 season—the Cubs' alleged curse involves a goat denied admission to the 1945 Series—but new manager Dusty Baker and a talented young pitching staff carried the Cubs to the N.L. Central title. After beating the Braves in the division series, Chicago jumped on Florida, winning three of the first four games and, after dropping game five, taking a 3-0 lead into the eighth inning of the potential pennant-clincher at Wrigley Field. That's when Chicago fan Steve Bartman, cheering his beloved team from a front-row seat down the leftfield line, instinctively reached for a foul fly ball—and inadvertently kept Cubs left fielder Moises Alou from catching it. There was no official interference (the ball was in the stands) and it should have been an innocuous footnote. Instead, batter Luis Castillo, given new life, walked. After four hits, a couple of walks, a critical error, and a sacrifice fly, an astonishing eight runs had crossed the plate. Thousands of fans jammed onto Wavefield and Sheffield Avenues, not to mention the 39,577 inside Wrigley Field, went home stunned. The Marlins won the next night, 9–6, to advance to the World Series.

Who's Responsible When a Player Dies?

On July 31, 2001, the Minnesota Vikings' 335-pound Pro Bowl lineman, Korey Stringer, collapsed during a training camp session held in the searing heat. His body temperature was 108.8 degrees when he arrived at a hospital, where Stringer died the following day.

Eighteen months later, in February 2003, Baltimore Orioles pitching prospect Steve Bechler died of heatstroke suffered during a spring training workout in Florida. The local medical examiner reported that a dietary supplement containing ephedra, which Bechler had been using, played a role in the tragedy. Ephedra was also implicated in Stringer's death, although there was no evidence that he used the substance.

The NFL, the NCAA, and the International Olympic Committee have banned ephedra, and Bechler's death led to calls for Major League Baseball to do the same. Congressional hearings were held in July 2003 regarding a total ban of the unregulated, over-the-counter substance. In 2004, President George Bush announced that the FDA was banning it.

Meanwhile, the families of both Bechler and Stringer went to court. Bechler's parents filed a wrongful death suit against the makers of the supplement, arguing that it was unsafe and the company was negligent. Stringer's widow sued the Vikings and the team doctor, holding them responsible for her husband's death. A judge dismissed her claims against the team, and she later settled with the doctor for an undisclosed sum.

Two Number Ones

Flash back to the 1997 college football season. The University of Michigan Wolverines, ranked number one in both polls, won the Rose Bowl on New Year's Day of 1998. But the Nebraska Cornhuskers won the Orange Bowl later that night, and the next day ascended to the top spot in the coaches' poll. Michigan and Nebraska shared the national title. After considerable hand-wringing, the Bowl Championship Series (BCS) was created the following spring (see page 77), ostensibly to create a national college championship game

The national championship game may have been born, but the controversy did not die. In 2000, one-loss Florida State was selected instead of one-loss Miami, a team it had lost to earlier in the year, to meet number-one Oklahoma in the title game. In 2001, one-loss Oregon was bypassed by one-loss Nebraska, a 62–36 loser in its conference title game, to face number-one Miami. But that was nothing compared to the 2003 college football season, when the one-loss University of Southern California (USC) Trojans, ranked number one in both the Associated Press and ESPN/*USA Today* polls, were bypassed for the Sugar Bowl (the game whose turn it was for the national-title game) by a complicated BCS formula that pitted the one-loss Louisiana State University (LSU) Tigers against the one-loss Oklahoma Sooners in that game. USC was left to play number-four Michigan in the Rose Bowl.

The BCS contract stipulated that the coaches in the ESPN/*USA Today* poll had to vote for the winner of the Sugar Bowl as the national champion. But the writers in the Associated Press poll were under no such obligation. So when USC beat Michigan 28-14 in the Rose Bowl on January 1, the Trojans wrapped up half of the national championship. LSU grabbed the other half three days later by stopping Oklahoma and its Heisman Trophy-winning quarterback, Jason White, 21–14.

Steroid Abuse

In February of 2004, the federal government indicted four men for illegally distributing steroids. One of the men was the personal trainer of record-setting slugger Barry Bonds (see box on page 104).

Neither Bonds—nor any other baseball player—was implicated in the charges, but even in a Presidential election year, the indictments put the incendiary issue of anabolic steroid abuse by athletes on the front pages of newspapers all across the country.

NASCAR Rides High

Far removed from its days as a regional sport that appealed mostly to the fans in the South, NASCAR continued in the new millennium to build on the tremendous growth it enjoyed in the 1990s. With popular stars such as Jeff Gordon (see page 66) and Dale Earnhardt Jr., plus crossover drivers such as 2002 champion Tony Stewart (a former Indy car star), stock car racing surged to new heights, with a broader fan base, record attendance, and increased television ratings.

Still, the sport was not about to ease up on the throttle. Alarmed by the 2003 season results, in which the title was taken by a driver, Matt Kenseth, who won just one race (Ryan Newman, meanwhile, won eight but finished sixth in the standings), NASCAR revamped its points system for 2004. More points are now awarded for winning a race. More importantly, the top 10 drivers after 26 of the season's 36 races are "restarted" with a preset number of points, essentially creating a playoff for the title—and, NASCAR hopes, even more fan interest.

2000–2003

It is illegal in the United States to possess anabolic steroids without a medical prescription, but athletes increasingly were suspected of utilizing the muscle builders to improve performance—whether that meant lifting greater weights, tackling harder, or hitting a baseball farther. Not only did steroid abuse alter the landscape of the level playing field, though, it also presented potentially harmful health concerns. "Steroids present a very significant and a very serious issue for this sport," baseball commissioner Bud Selig said early in 2004.

The issues were serious enough that Selig and players' union chief Donald Fehr were called before a Congressional committee in Washington, D.C. to testify. And in his 2004 State of the Union address, President George W. Bush called on athletes to be good role models and for sports organizations to work harder to ban steroids and other performance-enhancing drugs from being used.

These stories and more continue. New winners will be crowned, new records broken, new memories made. As this book and others in the Sports in America *series have shown, the role of athletic competition, especially spectator sports, has grown steadily in the past century to its place today as a vast web of influence upon just about every area of American life. As Larry Keith writes in the Foreword, "Sports does matter."*

Barry Busts Out

Barry Bonds

Early in a major league career that began with the Pittsburgh Pirates in 1986, Barry Bonds was a lithe speedster who could sometimes hit for power. But by the early 2000s, Bonds had transformed into a bulked-up slugger who had become the greatest home run hitter of his generation. Opposing managers became so fearful of Bonds that they began to routinely take the bat out of his hands, intentionally walking him in nearly every conceivable situation. After signing with the San Francisco Giants in 1993, Bonds averaged 39.8 home runs his first eight seasons. That hardly prepared anyone for his unbelievable outburst in 2001, when he hit 73 home runs, eclipsing the record 70 that Mark McGwire hit only three years earlier (see page 81). At age 38 in 2002, Bonds followed his record year with another 49 home runs; by the end of 2003, he was at 658 for his career, behind only Henry Aaron (755), Babe Ruth (714), and Willie Mays (660), Bonds' godfather, on baseball's all-time list.

Other Milestones of 2000–2004

2000

✔ On July 9, Pete Sampras won the men's singles title at Wimbledon to earn his 13th Grand Slam tennis title, surpassing Roy Emerson for the all-time career Grand Slam record.

✔ Controversial University of Indiana head basketball coach Bobby Knight was fired on September 10 after 29 seasons because of a "pattern of unacceptable behavior." On March 23, 2001, he was hired to coach at Texas Tech University.

✔ New York's first Subway Series in 44 years—and the first between the Yankees and Mets—was decided in game five at Shea Stadium on October 26. In the top of the ninth with the score tied, 2–2, Luis Sojo hit an RBI single off Mets starter Al Leiter, leading to a 4–2 win and the Yankees' record 26th world title.

✔ On December 11, All-Star shortstop Alex Rodriguez signed a 10-year, $252 million deal with the Texas Rangers, the biggest contract in sports history. In 2004 he was traded, at his request, to the New York Yankees for second baseman Alfonso Soriano.

2001

✔ Running great Jim Ryun's 36-year-old high school record in the mile (3:55.3, June 27, 1965) was snapped on May 27 by 18-year-old Alan Webb, who ran the distance in 3:53.43 at the Prefontaine Classic in Oregon.

✔ Ali and Frazier met again on June 8 at Turning Stone Casino in Verona, New York, when the daughters of the boxing rivals (Muhammad Ali and Joe

Pete Sampras

Frazier fought three of the most famous bouts in history in the 1970s) squared off. Laila Ali outlasted Jacqui Frazier-Lyde over eight rounds for the victory.

2002

✔ The first Olympic women's bobsled event, on February 19 in Salt Lake City, was even more historic when American Vonetta Flowers became the first black person to win an Olympic Winter Games gold medal, as she and teammate Jill Bakken claimed victory.

✔ The Los Angeles Lakers clinched their third straight NBA title on June 12 at the Continental Airlines Arena in East Rutherford, New Jersey, with a 113–107 win over the New Jersey Nets to complete a four-game sweep.

2003

✔ After beating the Lakers in the Western Conference semifinals and the Dallas Mavericks in the conference finals, the San Antonio Spurs eliminated the Nets in six games in the NBA Finals in June. An 88–77 home-court victory on June 15 at the SBC Center marked the Spurs' second NBA title.

2004

✔ On February 1, the New England Patriots beat the Carolina Panthers 32–29 in Super Bowl XXXVIII in Houston. The Patriots' Adam Vinatieri kicked a 41-yard field goal with four seconds left to decide the outcome. It was the second time in three seasons that the unflappable Vinatieri won a Super Bowl with a field goal (his 48-yard kick as time ran out beat the St. Louis Rams 20–17 in Super Bowl XXXVI in January of 2002).

RESOURCES

1990s and 2000s Events and Personalities

Barry Bonds: Baseball's Superman
By Steven Travers (Champaign, Illinois: Sports Publishing LLC, 2002)
By the early 2000s, the Giants' outfielder had become a slugger feared by opposing pitchers more than any other player since the legendary Babe Ruth.

Post-Cold War America (1992–present)
By James Haley, Editor (San Diego, California: Greenhaven Press, 2003)
The various articles in this book look at topics that have shaped recent American history, including the tragic events of September 11, 2001.

On the Course With . . . Tiger Woods
By Matt Christopher (New York: Little Brown & Company, 1998)
A look at the golfing superstar's life from one of America's most prolific writers about sports for kids and young adults.

Young Superstars of Tennis: the Venus and Serena Williams Story
By Mike Fillon (Greensboro, North Carolina: Avisson Press, 1999)
With style and grace off the court and powerful play on it, the Williams sisters took the tennis world by storm near the turn of the century.

American Sports History

The Complete Book of the Olympics
By David Wallechinsky (New York: Viking Penguin, 2000)
An extremely detailed look at every Winter and Summer Olympics from 1896 to the present, including complete lists of medal winners and short biographies of important American and international athletes.

The Encyclopedia of North American Sports History
Edited by Ralph Hickok (New York: Facts On File, 1992)
This title includes articles on the origins of all the major sports as well as capsule biographies of key figures.

Encyclopedia of Women and Sport in America
Edited by Carol Oglesby et al. (Phoenix: Oryx Press, 1998)
A large overview of not only key female personalities on and off the playing field, but a look at issues surrounding women and sports.

Encyclopedia of World Sport
Edited by David Levinson and Karen Christensen (New York: Oxford University Press, 1999)
This wide-ranging book contains short articles on an enormous variety of sports, personalities, events, and issues, most of which have some connection to American sports history. This is a great starting point for additional research.

ESPN SportsCentury

Edited by Michael McCambridge
(New York: Hyperion, 1999)
Created to commemorate the 20th century in sports, this book features essays by well-known sportswriters as well as commentary by popular ESPN broadcasters. Each decade's chapter features an in-depth story about the key event of that time period.

Facts and Dates of American Sports

By Gordon Carruth and Eugene Ehrlich
(New York: Harper & Row, 1988)
Very detailed look at sports history, focusing on when events occurred. Large list of birth and death dates for major figures.

Sports of the Times

By David Fischer and William Taafe.
(New York: Times Books, 2003)
A unique format tracks the top sports events on each day of the calendar year. Find out the biggest event for every day from January 1 to December 31.

Total Baseball

Edited by John Thorn, Pete Palmer, and Michael Gershman. (New York: Total Sports, 2004, eighth edition)
The indispensable bible of baseball, it contains the career records of every Major Leaguer. Essays in the front of the book cover baseball history, team history, overviews of baseball in other countries, and articles about the role of women and minorities in the game.

Total Football

Edited by Bob Carroll, John Thorn, Craig Neft, and Michael Gershman
(New York: HarperCollins, 2000)
The complete and official record of every player who has played in the NFL. The huge book also contains essays on a wide variety of topics relating to pro football.

Sports History Web Sites

ESPN.com

www.sports.espn.go.com
The Web site run by the national cable sports channel contains numerous history sections within each sport. This one for baseball is the largest and includes constantly updated statistics on baseball.

Hickok Sports

www.hickoksports.com
Not the most beautiful site and devoid of pictures, but filled with a wealth of information on sports at all levels. It is run by Ralph Hickok, an experienced sportswriter, and is regularly updated with the latest winners.

Official League Web Sites

www.nfl.com
www.nba.com
www.mlb.com
www.nhl.com
Each of the major sports leagues has history sections on their official Web sites

Official Olympics Web Site

http://www.olympic.org/uk/games/index_uk.asp
Complete history of the Olympic Games, presented by the International Olympic Committee.

The Sporting News "Vault"

www.sportingnews.com/archives
More than 100 years old, The St. Louis-based Sporting News is the nation's oldest sports weekly. In the history section of its Web site, it has gathered hundreds of articles on sports events, championships, stars, and more. It also includes audio clips of interviews with top names in sports from yesterday and today.

INDEX